BASEBALL LIKE IT OUGHTA BE

HOW A SHOE SALESMAN'S MADISON MALLARDS AND HIS RENEGADE STAFF IGNITED THE SUMMER-COLLEGIATE BASEBALL REVOLUTION

TOM ALESIA

August Publications

August Publications
215 10th Av. S., Unit 621
Minneapolis, MN 55415
augustpublications.com

Visit Tom Alesia's website at *TomWriteTurns.com*.

All photos courtesy Madison Mallards unless otherwise noted.

Library of Congress Control Number: 2025930149

ISBN 978-1-938532-88-7 (Print)

ISBN 978-1-938532-89-4 (eBook)

10 9 8 7 6 5 4 3 2 1

Designer (cover): Kyle Chisholm

CONTENTS

To Susan and Mark

FOREWORD
JOHN KOVALIC

"Baseball Like it Oughta Be."

It's a classic adage (the '86 Mets used it, as did the '96 Cardinals), and one the Madison Mallards adopted from the very start.

If the cleats fit....

Though I missed the Madison Mallards' 2001 inaugural season, I'd made it to several prior Madison minor-league games over the years. All were...fine. Fun, even, at times. My first Mallards game, though? It was unlike anything I'd seen at Warner Park—aka "The Duck Pond"—before.

These weren't professional players, but college kids getting a little extra summer baseball in: talented teens who wanted to improve, kids capable of incredible plays (with the occasional spectacular flub). They were there for the love of the game. The crowds that quickly grew loved them for it.

But it was so much more.

Maynard and the Kovalic family. Maynard's on the left.

To keep fans entertained, Mallards management had cooked up a seemingly endless stream of between-inning antics: Diaper Derbies with babies crawling for honor and glory; Bat Spins where (mainly) dudes stumbled perilously off-balance across the field; Beer Batters who—should they strike out—halved the price of pours; T-shirt tosses, yes, but also brat tosses, cheese curd tosses…if it wasn't tied down, it was probably tossed to the crowd at some point during a Mallards season; Victory Balls at the end of a winning nine innings; Maynard G. Mallard zip-lining from the outfield to home plate to begin every game; and of course the now-iconic cry of "WIENER" whenever a ball was fouled into the stands (grab it for a free hot dog)!

It was exciting and exhilarating and quite brilliant.

Other teams had run similar promotions, but nobody had ever put them all together in such a wondrous, frantic whole.

Mallards management cared deeply about their guests and it showed, with exceptional service and respect for everyone who walked through their gates. The team behind the scenes was just as focused as the ones on the field to the fan experience. Best of all: a Mallards game was (and remains) affordable.

It's that sort of commitment that led me to:

- Select season ticket seats while the renovated ballpark was still under construction one snowy spring morning in 2011 (I kept the hard hat with the Mallards logo on it—don't tell).
- Experience both the world's Largest First Pitch *and* the world's largest Old Fashioned (fortunately during different games).
- Witness the night the team drew 10,000 fans, breaking all kinds of records (and possibly a city ordinance or two—attendance was afterwards capped).
- Scarf down pork-laced hot fudge sundaes during "Bacon Appreciation Days," and wait hours for a rain-delayed frog-leg-eating competition one year when the Green Bay Bullfrogs came to town.
- Smash printers on the field with baseball bats for *Office Space* night.
- Celebrate wildly as the team captured a couple of Northwoods League championships.
- Play catch with my kid in the outfield, and run the bases with them.

Of all these memories and more, the ones with my child will forever be my favorites.

Apart from anything else—apart from the "All you care to eat and drink" Duck Blind and the Beer Batters, who can be ridiculously generous with their strikeouts—the Mallards are an organization devoted first and foremost to kids and to families.

The Duck Pond is a *very* special place, these days.

Tom Alesia has perfectly captured the magic that is the Madison Mallards experience in *Baseball Like it Oughta Be*, a thoroughly researched and exceedingly readable history of the team. It's chock-full of compelling tidbits (some new to even me, a confessed "Super Fan") and insights from those who were there at the start of it all.

In short, once you pick up *Baseball Like it Oughta Be*, it's an awfully difficult book to put down. It's a sparkling, well-written, comprehensive tale of one of the great baseball success stories of the past 25 years...or, frankly, ever.

Like the Madison Mallards themselves, it's just dang fun.

It's a baseball story like it oughta be.

—John Kovalic, February 2025

John Kovalic is an internationally recognized and multi-award-winning cartoonist, game designer, and writer. He helped create the revolutionary party game, Apples to Apples, *and is responsible for the look of the perennial best-selling* Munchkin *card game (he's drawn more than 7,000 cards for the game). John was inducted into the Games Manufacturers of America Hall of Fame in 2004. In his spare time, John can be found in Section 103 at the Duck Pond, root, root, rooting for the Mallards.*

CHAPTER 1
THE 10,061-FAN GAME

Playing catch at the ballpark.

SPRING BARELY MADE AN APPEARANCE IN MADISON, Wisconsin in 2004, between the lingering winter and early summer. When sun-drenched skies and savory mid-70s temperatures arrived on Saturday evening, June 12, the state capital's summer-collegiate baseball team—the Madison

Mallards, comprised of players scattered at schools nation-wide—hosted Minnesota's Rochester Honkers. Part of the 11-year-old Northwoods League, these Midwest teams with scrappy marketing featured rosters with competitors seeking to reach the lowest rung on professional baseball's long, wobbly ladder.

For decades, summer-collegiate baseball was largely the domain of charming and quiet outposts in Cape Cod, Alaska, and across Middle America. Soon, many wide-eyed summer-collegiate leagues, imitating the Northwoods' revelry, sprouted across the country, mixing the sport with off-the-field, off-the-wall entertainment.

And the Mallards led them.

To MARK the single game that helped fuel this evolution, one needs to look at that Mallards-Honkers contest at Madison's Warner Park in 2004. That was when an astounding 10,061 fans—still a summer-collegiate attendance record—over-flowed a patchwork ballpark, lovingly dubbed the Duck Pond. The ballpark's nickname was created by the Mallards' tireless owner and shoe salesman marvel Steve Schmitt, who bought the new team on a whim during a tumultuous personal period in February 2001. Years later, it's still called the Duck Pond and, after annual remodeling—where the Mallards funnel considerable profits and smartly conceived promotions—offers a carnival midway's bells and whistles with vibes like a daily Oktoberfest. Competitive baseball is the show, but the Mallards' clever hijinks is the jubilant attraction. Bright yellow and green mascot Maynard, for instance, arrives by zipline each game from a four-story right-field party perch to home plate.

The Mallards already had established themselves in 2004 as the standard bearer to a growing number of for-profit summer-collegiate teams trying to create fan frenzy. There were approximately 10 nonprofit leagues in 1994, and that tally—with some teams trying to make money in the oft-precarious baseball business—jumped to almost 40 leagues by 2008. Entering the 2025 season, more than 80 summer-collegiate leagues were set, ranging from competition in western Canada to Puerto Rico. All 50 states have at least one team in one of these leagues. The leagues vary significantly in their approach and financing: some use the Northwoods' for-profit model; others require players to pay between $1,300 and $1,500 to join a team; a few stay in one city where teams play every game; and about one dozen nonprofit entities remain, including the Cape Cod League, partially funded by MLB. More than 600 teams participate. That means the Pineville Porcupines, Hastings Sodbusters, Wenatchee AppleSox, Augusta Surgin' Sturgeon and *so many* other teams will seek summer-collegiate players and supporters. Remarkably, the Mallards seemingly bottled their fans' enthusiasm more than 20 years ago. As they approached 25 years old in late May 2025, the team drew more than 4.3 million fans in team history. Also, the Mallards routinely averaged more than 6,000 fans per game and 200,000-plus attendees annually, easily leading the nation's summer-collegiate leagues in total attendance each season since 2002. They don't rest on their laurels. They often don't rest, period.

How do the Mallards maintain that popular momentum?

Well, *that's* the Duck Pond miracle.

Maynard's iconic entrance on the zipline.

LESS THAN TWO weeks before that 2004 Mallards-Honkers'
game, the Mallards entered their fourth season in the Northwoods League with a sluggish road trip, losing five of six
games, through unassuming Upper Midwest towns with long
baseball histories: Wausau, St. Cloud and Alexandria. The
Mallards then played their home opener at the city's northside
Warner Park.

Schmitt's purchase of the Mallards required a $150,000
franchise fee to the Northwoods League, and the team
succeeded after three Madison professional baseball franchises largely stumbled across 20 years of empty seats, annual
financial losses, inadequate facilities and plunging fan interest. The city's notorious party-hearty residents became jaded
toward baseball teams in a shoddy ballpark. So, when the
Mallards debuted on June 2, 2001, Madison's collective yawn

toward the new team could drown out the cracks of the team's wood bats.

However, when life gives Schmitt lemons, he makes, well, lemon meringue pie.

In spring 2001, with his tiny staff and a few friends, he painted the entire gray ballpark into a garish maze of green, gold and red. Along with dynamic marketing director Vern Stenman, just 23 and barely out of St. Cloud State University, they practically begged fans to attend a Mallards game. The team often offered free entry to anyone wearing a Milwaukee Brewers cap—a common hat, given that Madison was 76 miles from then-Miller Park, the Brewers' spiffy new ballpark —or told anyone from, say, Sun Prairie, a sizable Madison suburb, to show their ID and enter without paying admission. Crowds arrived, not immediately but eventually.

With that 1-5 record in 2004, the Mallards entered their season's first home series. One year before, the Mallards became surprising mighty ducks at the box office, and Madison's dreary winters gave residents pent-up energy for summer's outdoor good times. The Mallards went bonkers while presenting traditional baseball with all of the sport's sudden thrills and frequent lulls. They mixed between-inning tomfoolery, having youngsters, for instance, racing to dress in oversized uniforms; anything-goes giveaways (freebies ranged from glow-in-the-dark baseballs and ceramic beer steins to full-sized bats and nose jobs); cheap beer—two-for-one Budweiser on Tuesdays and many tap bargains—and general-admission tickets for $5, or $3 for kids and seniors. Sponsors craved the Mallards' crowd: families, groups on a workplace outing, revelers, scores of Little League players, and adults enjoying a low-cost game. Young and old. All bases were covered on demographics.

On a dreary Wednesday night, June 9, 2004, against the Mankato MoonDogs, the Mallards still attracted nearly 5,200 fans, a remarkable tally among summer-collegiate teams where crowds of 1,000 were celebrated as financial successes. A proudly liberal city, Madison jumped aboard the Mallards' zany bandwagon, creating an atmosphere that made the much-heralded, dominant University of Wisconsin teams seem somewhat staid. The Mallards became a rite of summer—at first, a curiosity and, eventually, a tradition. The 2004 season's home opener featured bubbly promotions, but the team's shrewd and successful manager Darrell Handelsman provided the most entertainment.

And so began one of the Mallards' most memorable and influential home stands in their astounding 25-year history.

With the game tied at 1, Handelsman sprang from the dugout when Madison's batter, still in the batter's box, was called out after his swing caused the ball to graze his chest, then inch into play. It should have been called a foul ball, but the base umpire called him out. (Northwoods League games at the time featured two umpires: one behind the plate and one patrolling the bases.)

Handelsman launched himself like a cannonball toward the base umpire. He shouted at the umpire, Matt Phillips, then turned his cap backwards, shifting the Mallards' wacky duck logo, so he could shout at the ump within a couple of inches from his face. Knowing his team needed a kick in the pants, Handelsman wanted the outburst to motivate his players. The base umpire, though, did not eject him as the manager continued to bark. Adding to an unusual atmosphere: During the entire brouhaha the song "Hava Nagila" blared over the loudspeakers—due to a request made by Handelsman to have the folk tune played during any home entanglement with the blues.

"I kept waiting for somebody to come get me, the home-plate umpire or anybody," Handelsman said. "They just let me keep wearing the ump out."

Handelsman eventually eased his verbal venom, and that was when home-plate umpire Tommy Crenshaw walked over to Handelsman and ejected him.

As he left the field, though, Handelsman stopped at home plate, regained his fury and kept kicking dirt. Mallards fans delighted considerably in the Earl Weaver-style tantrum, giving Handelsman a raucous ovation when he finally walked leisurely and defiantly toward the dugout.

Schmitt believed word of mouth spoke volumes about the Mallards' success. Though a hardcore baseball devotee, Schmitt understood some fans did not give a hoot about the Mallards' wins and losses. The fans, however, wanted to be entertained—and Handelsman did it unintentionally. Did Handelsman's tirade prompt word of mouth? Absolutely. Fans describing Handelsman's rage kept the Mallards in conversations outside the park for days afterwards.

By early June 2004, Mallards officials harnessed every opportunity to excite fans. Foul balls, for instance, provoked cries of "wiener" from Mallards public address announcer Rich Reynolds, alerting fans that the ball could be returned for a free hot dog. The one-word response later became a popular Mallards T-shirt, and fans often yelled "wiener" before the announcer did. ("Wiener" is *still* used by PA announcers at Mallards' games, and it was a prominent part of the team's 2024 marketing on city buses.) Baseball, though, was played seriously and vigorously. Talented collegiate players, as eager as puppies to become professionals, often bonded tightly for one summer wanting to attract scouts' attention and, given their competitiveness, to vie for a league title. Handelsman's home-opener rage worked perfectly as motivation, and his players responded with a three-run victory.

The next night after that 2004 home opener, rain postponed the Mallards game. On Friday, June 11, about 2,900 fans, kept low by harsh weather, watched the team's victory.

Then Mallards mania rose to new heights on June 12, 2004.

Wiener!

THAT DAY, the Duck Pond's gates opened at 5:35 p.m., 90 minutes before the first pitch, and lines were already longer than a deep home run, extending past a nearby football and soccer field. Nearly 1,200 parking spaces at the sizable Warner Park lot filled quickly, so fans started taking spots at the strip mall across busy North Sherman Avenue.

More and more and more fans arrived. Stenman—who often slept overnight in the team's makeshift offices to work nearly around the clock—and his staff knew the game would draw a big crowd because a giant health care company, one of a growing number of Mallards' sponsors, bought more than 4,000 tickets for their employees.

Madison resident Dennis Degenhardt and his wife, Linda, attended the game. They served as one of 20 or so host families to Mallards players during the 2004 season. Host families, which let players stay with them in their homes at no cost, were imperative to every summer-collegiate league because the players were unpaid due to stringent NCAA rules.

On that Saturday night, the Degenhardts arrived early at the Duck Pond and immediately noticed the burgeoning crowd. Dennis was amazed and thought, "Good God, where did all of these people come from?"

By game time, Mallards starting pitcher Billy Phillips was understandably nervous due to the massive crowd. Phillips, from Division II Emporia State University in Emporia, Kansas, allowed one run in the top of the first inning before he settled in and earned the 4-1 win. "My school is small," Phillips said afterward. "A hundred people at a game."

That night, about 6,000 fans were expected. It was the Mallards' 100th home game, and to commemorate that milestone the Mallards distributed prints of the Duck Pond. They were gone as quickly as a steal of second base.

Another part of the Mallards' typical oddball promotions that night, the team welcomed colorful ex-big leaguer Jay Johnstone—with no ties to Wisconsin but one of Schmitt's many friends—to sign autographs and throw out the first pitch. Johnstone retired from baseball in 1985, so his appearance was aimed at the Mallards' handful of baseball fanatics.

Instead, by their fourth season, the Mallards became a must-see attraction—affordable and entertaining with endless pre-social media buzz—despite competing with the city's many summertime options.

By mid-game on June 12, 2004, with Mallards staff scrambling to handle an overflow crowd, that Saturday night's official attendance was announced: 10,061.

Unimaginable.

The Mallards outdrew the Tampa Bay Devil Rays' crowd from the night before. They outdrew each of the Montreal Expos' next four home games. And they outdrew every minor-league team that night.

Various caps on capacity over many years prevented the Mallards from drawing more than 7,500 fans again. So, Mallards staff and fans have embraced that 10,000-plus night as tightly as seams on a baseball.

After that game, Handelsman, a Northwoods League manager since 1997, marveled: "I never thought in all my years, I'd ever see something like that."

The game's attendance still stands as a national amateur summer-collegiate league record by 2,500 people—breaking a year-old record held by…the 2003 Mallards.

Careful what you wish for, though. The game's crowd overwhelmed the box office, concession stands, souvenir outlets and bathrooms. At one point, team officials considered using rope inside the right-field playing area to allow more room for fans and, basically, creating a human outfield "fence." (In retrospect, Stenman felt they should have done that. Placing fans behind a rope to manage an overflow crowd was one of the great traditions in baseball, but had not been done for many decades.) The fans' wait for food and beer meant at least a couple of innings standing beneath the Duck Pond's stands; and one concession line extended from under the seats behind home plate to more than halfway up left field.

Workers were frantic, but Schmitt and Stenman walked along the lines, giving out free tickets and concession vouchers while apologizing to fans for the wait. There was not a clear, official capacity at the Duck Pond because one had never been needed for the previous 25 years.

Surprisingly, the fans' reaction, Stenman said, was not anger. Instead, he received no complaints afterwards.

"I talked to a lot of fans that night. Because of the lines, we gave them free stickers, tickets to another game, beer tokens, anything. I kept saying, 'Sorry the line's so long,'" Stenman said. "But the mood to many of them about the huge crowd was, 'This is really cool.' It meant that we had figured out what baseball was going to be in Madison. The people that were there that night understood that, and they were willing to give us a chance. All of a sudden, it was the symbol of what would come."

In the weeks that followed, Madison's city officials cut capacity at the Mallards' Duck Pond for safety purposes. Twenty years after that game, Schmitt said simply about the enormous crowd, "We weren't ready." The city's fire department limited the Duck Pond to 5,000 fans—an overreaction given that the sizable park could handle up to 8,000 fans. By early August, city officials agreed to increase the ballpark's capacity to 7,500 after the Mallards installed three 20-foot exit gates. Two weeks later, in the Duck Pond, the Mallards won their first Northwoods League title.

More amazing was what happened next: The Mallards never lost their unmatched popularity among summer-collegiate teams.

Ever.

Year after year after year, the Mallards pulled a rabbit out of their ball cap. Each season, the Mallards never took their fans' support for granted, even if they could have switched to autopilot before Obama's first administration.

The heavily hyped Savannah Bananas formed in 2016 as a summer-collegiate team after the city's loss of Minor League Baseball before abandoning that level in August 2022. They became a traveling pro baseball circus with countless antics, including players performing dance routines, and left traditional baseball in the dust. The Bananas' "fans first" marketing battle cry is practically identical to the Mallards' debut philosophy in 2001.

Ckyler Tengler, celebrating a 2024 win.

But the Mallards predate the Bananas by 15 years— thriving without going bananas on the field. It is plain old, traditional baseball, a cumbersome sport with flashes of excitement. The Mallards dress up every aspect around that game. Between the third and fourth innings, for example, two fans in jumbo, well-padded bubbles race toward each other from opposite sides of second base to knock the other person down—and it's sponsored by the Wisconsin Department of Transportation.

The Mallards, expected to be dead on arrival in 2001— and they almost were—succeeded so far beyond expectations that they are the envy of countless sports franchises seeking even a morsel of their popular and financial success.

How? Why? What?

The Mallards story follows an owner's obsession; the dreamland of a young marketing director, who quit an NHL front office job; relentless customer service for their fans; fresh promotions annually; belief in what many viewed as a struggling neighborhood; and the embracement of America's least likely renowned ballpark.

Welcome to the Duck Pond.

CHAPTER 2
CREATING THE NORTHWOODS LEAGUE

Dick Radatz Jr., left. Photo courtesy Northwoods League.

DICK RADATZ JR. SPENT HIS CHILDHOOD SURROUNDED BY baseball. His father, Dick Radatz—a 6-foot-6, 230-pound relief pitcher, nicknamed the Monster (a moniker he disliked) —played four impressive seasons with the Boston Red Sox from 1962 to 1965. In 1964, Radatz set the MLB record for strikeouts in a season by a relief pitcher with 181 K's, a record that still stands. A two-time All-Star during that time, Radatz continued to pitch in the major leagues for various teams until 1969. With Boston, Radatz brought Dick Jr., the oldest of Radatz's three children and his only son, to participate in the Red Sox's father-son games in Fenway Park. As a five- and six-year-old boy in full uniform, Dick Jr. charmed fans and photographers with his cute intensity and surprising aptitude at bat.

Named to the Red Sox's Hall of Fame in 1997, Radatz also earned acclaim for his success at stopping Mickey Mantle, striking out the legendary slugger 12 of the 16 times that they faced each other.

The younger Radatz played baseball at Albion College in Michigan, where he was the team's captain. But a broken collarbone and separated shoulder injuries ended any professional aspirations. He then studied at Ohio University, earning a master's degree in Sports Administration.

In 1982, he joined the Los Angeles Dodgers' office staff, operating the Dodgertown spring-training facility in Vero Beach, Florida. A year later, at 24, he became general manager of the Boston Red Sox's Class-A minor-league team in Winter Haven, Florida. He was successful there, receiving the Florida State League's executive of the year honor in 1986. Three years later, though, his comments to the press concerning Winter Haven Red Sox players' attitudes during a combined won-loss record of 97-181 in the 1988-89 seasons, in part, prompted his exit from the team.

Radatz shifted to associate director of Michigan Special

Olympics. But baseball was his passion. And an idea that he
mulled as far back as the late 1980s—a for-profit Midwestern
summer-collegiate league—stuck with him. The idea
stemmed from seeing the success of the University of Miami
baseball team, which drew thousands of fans each spring with
flashy marketing.

Working with George MacDonald, Jr., former president of
the Florida State League for 18 seasons, Radatz sought to
create a new type of summer-collegiate league. He envisioned
a business plan dramatically different from the high-brow and
talent-rich Cape Cod League, a summer pipeline for amateur
players to the big leagues since 1923. The Cape Cod League
featured 10 teams tucked together in the upscale Mass-
achusetts tourist spot and competed in games with no admission price, some lawn-chair seating and pass-the-hat
donations. All the teams were within one hour of each other.

A Michigan native, Radatz eyed the Midwest for his collegiate for-profit league. He knew many Midwest cities and
towns could not support minor league team. But these places
still had well-aged, roomy ballparks, and local governments
eager to offer low-priced summer entertainment.

In June 1994, the five-team Northwoods League, using
wood bats to mimic the minor-league experience, debuted
with four co-founders: Radatz, MacDonald, Bill McKee and
John Wendel. Radatz pushed hard on the Northwoods
League's success. To start the league, he borrowed from his
wife's 401(k) account to get on the road and secure leases in
Kenosha and Wausau, Wisconsin.

The Northwoods League lost $33,000 in its first season,
requiring league officials to accept a deal with one of their
stockholders who covered that debt—then charged 10 percent
interest. (The league did not fully pay back that loan until

1999.) About 68,000 fans attended Northwoods League games in 1994—or under 300 people per contest.

"If we had a good night in Wausau (Wisconsin)," Radatz recalled, "we had to get that money down to Dubuque (Iowa) to pay those bills."

Radatz said he experienced many "sleepless nights." He had too much money and time invested to give up. The league "was inspiration and desperation in how this came about," he said on the Northwoods League's weekly TV show in 2019. "We needed jobs. We were looking for work."

Would small Midwest communities rally around a league filled with college players aspiring to become minor leaguers? Some did.

The pioneering five Northwoods League teams in Wisconsin, Iowa and Minnesota were: Dubuque Mud Puppies, Rochester Honkers, Kenosha Kroakers, Wausau (later Wisconsin) Woodchucks and Manitowoc Skunks.

In the ensuing years, the Northwoods League continued to stumble, even without having to pay their collegiate players. The Mud Puppies drew about one hundred fans on "a good night" to a ballpark near the Mississippi River, according to Robb Quinlan, a University of Minnesota player who joined the Mud Puppies in 1996.

Even before that, in 1997, when the Honkers' ballpark— across the way from the league headquarters in Rochester— needed a new women's bathroom, Radatz and team officials built it at nearly one-tenth the cost of outsourcing the project.

"I had a jackhammer in my hand," Radatz said. "I had a cement saw, we had the masks on, there was dust in my hair. We got this done for $7,000. It epitomized sweat equity."

Slowly, the Northwoods League expanded, and two of its five original home cities remained part of the league's core.

Radatz uncovered other markets where costs were low, ball-parks were available after the departure of MiLB and indy ball, and relationships between team and town developed financial bonds. Cities committed to fixing up vintage neighborhood ballparks in cities like Wausau and Mankato.

Many cities attracted more apathy than fans. Brainerd and Grand Forks failed, but Willmar survived. The Northwoods League began to form a strong core when Waterloo, La Crosse and Eau Claire gained faithful followings.

Radatz's idea began working. Slowly.

OPTIMISM HAD ALWAYS CREPT ALONG. In 1995, Waterloo's Midwest League team eventually relocated to Lansing, Michigan after a brief stop in Springfield, Illinois. The new Class-A Lansing Lugnuts sold $1 million in merchandise and finalized a nice naming-rights deal *before* their first game, leading Radatz to wonder, "How can we get some of that?" Although Lansing was a team with professional players, even if they were at a minor-league level, that marketing success could inspire Northwoods League teams to make money.

In addition, Radatz was able to expand into St. Cloud, Minnesota in 1997, marking a huge victory for the Northwoods League over fading professional independent leagues. St. Cloud attorney Harry Burns wanted to bring a professional independent team to the city with the Prairie League. City officials, though, sided with Radatz and picked the Northwoods League as the best entity to succeed in St. Cloud.

Burns fumed, "The city is refusing to go big time," and he added about the Northwoods League that "you're watching college kids you've never heard of, or never will hear from again."

St. Cloud officials chose correctly. The Prairie League, burdened by the weight of player salaries, folded in 1997; St. Cloud, meanwhile, remained a Northwoods League staple nearly 30 seasons later.

Then, in 1999, the first Northwoods League alum made the major leagues when 1995 Dubuque Mud Puppies pitcher Jeff Weaver started for the Detroit Tigers against the Minnesota Twins, allowing one hit in five innings. Following Weaver: Juan Pierre (Manitowoc Skunks), Jay Gibbons (Manitowoc Skunks), Curtis Granderson (Mankato Mashers) and the aforementioned Robb Quinlan.

Another boost to the Northwoods League was their season dates: Memorial Day weekend to mid-August. "April and May (weather) killed baseball in the Upper Midwest. We've brought it back," Radatz said. "We've built a better mousetrap."

In the mid-1990s, some communities—including Madison —opted for professional independent league teams, whose players were paid. Radatz scoffed at these teams. He called the Northern League (later the American Association), with teams in lucrative suburbs and midsized cities, as being "full of has-beens and wannabes. We are the up-and-comers."

Northern League commissioner Miles Wolff, also the founder of a similar summer-collegiate league in the form of the Carolinas' Coastal Plain League, took the high road, to a degree, in his view of the Northwoods League.

"Dick Radatz runs a great league. It may be the best of the college leagues," Wolff said in 2018. "His model works best for Dick Radatz. The league office gets a bigger cut of everything."

The Northwoods League received five percent of each team's gross. That money paid for advanced ticketing systems, flashy websites, vital league-wide stability, live game streaming and business-savvy league officials, including Radatz.

In late December 2000, Radatz landed the Northwoods League's biggest game changer in the form of a Madison team. The Black Wolf's departure occurred just as an opening in the Northwoods League happened when the Minot Green-heads struggled through their one and only season. On January 3, 2001—two weeks after a snowstorm cancelled a city meeting expected to finalize the deal—the Northwoods League landed in Madison.

Despite its growing population and comfortable mix of state government, thriving companies and a major university, Madison had a rough history with baseball. The Northwoods League team approval was buried deep in the morning news-paper's meeting story.

Initially, Radatz considered owning the team himself. After six weeks Radatz identified a Madison-based owner: the friendly, workaholic Steve Schmitt, the mastermind of a massively successful rural shoe store called The Shoe Box.

CHAPTER 3
STEVE SCHMITT, SHOE SAVANT

STEVE SCHMITT'S FATHER, BILL, GREW UP NEAR THE University of Wisconsin-Madison, where Bill's parents owned a family diner called the Snowflake Lunch. From 1920 to 1922, a regular customer was a young university student named Charles Lindbergh.

During high school, Bill cleaned tables at the restaurant. After graduating, he worked at UW Hospital, assisting patients using artificial limbs. Bill also drove a cab. A co-worker and friend set up Bill on a blind date with Janette Hefty, who lived near Madison in the minuscule village of Arena. They were married before the United States entered World War II, and Bill soon joined the Army Air Corps in 1942.

Later in the war, Bill spent considerable time on the remote but strategically invaluable island of Tinian in the Pacific Ocean. In early August 1945, Bill saw the Enola Gay, a B-29 bomber with Col. Paul Tibbets and his crew, being loaded for a confidential mission. Bill also observed the plane's return from their mission: They dropped an atomic bomb on Hiroshima.

With his mother's camera, Bill took photos of the Enola Gay as it taxied on the runway when he recognized the plane with its prominent "82" on it.

"Get the hell out of here," an MP shouted to Bill.

When the MP left, Bill took numerous pictures. Slightly more than 50 years later, Steve Schmitt sent Tibbets eight photos, including one of Schmitt's 2005 visit to a small monument on the largely forgotten but historic Tinian. Some of Bill's pictures are signed by Tibbets and displayed at Schmitt's shoe store. One photo is signed with a remarkably detailed inscription, "Paul Tibbets, pilot, B29 Enola Gay to Hiroshima 6 Aug. 1945." Tibbets, who died in 2007, rarely included "Hiroshima" with his signatures.

Bill Schmitt, Steve's father.
Photo courtesy Steve Schmitt.

Like countless other war veterans, Bill suffered debilitating after-effects from observing many atrocities. When he was released from duty in late 1945, his captain offered to put him on a plane heading to San Diego. Bill declined the flight.

"Can I go on a ship?" Bill asked.

He had seen so many airplane crashes that he felt safer returning to America on water. And even that was not secure; the ship, with Bill on board, spent five days from Tinian to

San Diego and needed to zig zag its route out of fear from enemy submarines potentially on the way to Tinian.

After returning from active duty, Bill, like other soldiers, faced demons from war experiences when he lived with Janette in Black Earth, a small village 21 miles west of Madison.

Then, on Feb. 8, 1947, Bill and Janette welcomed their only child, Steve. It was a sobering experience—literally—for Bill, who quit drinking the day Steve was born.

The birth was bittersweet. Janette had been diagnosed with tuberculosis (TB), forcing her to live in a Madison sanatorium until Steve was five years old.

For more than five years, Janette received treatment and lived at the Lake View Sanato-

Janette Hefty, Steve's mother. Photo courtesy Steve Schmitt.

rium, a 20,000-square-foot brick building in Madison. She had no verbal contact with her son. Instead, they waved at each other from Janette's second-story window weekly as their only communication.

"I got a lump in my throat," Steve said of those visits, "and I was too young to know why."

The former sanatorium building remains. From the Madison Mallards' home plate, the building is visible about one half-mile away. When Schmitt discussed his devotion to maintain the Duck Pond, the Mallards' home ballpark, Schmitt always mentioned pride for Madison's northside, noting the former factories of Oscar Mayer, which closed its giant Madison plant in 2017, nearly four decades removed from its peak of 4,000 employees, and other major factories. He also spoke about the neighborhood residents' resilience. All are true. But it was also the place that cured his mother.

Bill lived to be 93, while Steve's mom, Janette, lived until age 92 in 2009, dying seven weeks after Bill did. They were married more than 70 years. The couple attended numerous Mallards games, with Bill always wearing Mallards apparel. Looming in the distance and virtually unchanged on the exterior since the late 1940s was the nearby sanatorium, now used as the Dane County Department of Human Services offices with a sizable sled hill.

Add that personal twist—in a way, often difficult to express—when Steve acknowledged his desire to make the Duck Pond thrive at its oft-struggling location.

STEVE LIVED AS A BABY, toddler and young boy with his aunt and uncle in nearby Mazomanie, although Steve's father, Bill, worked in Black Earth and visited his young son often at noon, arriving on an old motor scooter. Steve's aunt and uncle ran a cheese factory in Mazomanie. Steve was the youngest of his three cousins living in their household.

In late 1952, Janette, who was released from the sanatorium, and Bill took Steve back and became a family in Black Earth.

Bill bought shoe repair equipment from a war widow, and he fixed shoes out of a Quonset hut, barely bigger than a chicken coop. Later, he opened Bill's Shoe and Sports Store in Black Earth's downtown. It started slowly. "After rainstorms," Steve said, "all three of us would go out with coffee cans and pick up nightcrawlers and sell them the next day for 15 cents a dozen."

Bill's Shoe and Sports Store offered everything from guns to vacuum cleaners to sporting goods. At first, Bill fixed shoes, but he did not think selling shoes would work. A friend from the posh Milwaukee suburb of Whitefish Bay convinced him to try it.

"He finally put some shoes in and all hell broke loose," Steve said. "I was probably 10 at the time. He put some shoes in the Quonset hut, and he quickly grew out of that location. He bought a building in Black Earth's downtown and opened a larger shop because of the shoes."

The roots of a colossal shoe store, still growing, were planted.

Steve Schmitt at Bill's Shoe Shop, his dad's store in Black Earth. Photo courtesy Steve Schmitt.

As a child, Steve—nicknamed Itch (something that stuck through his lifetime) by a teen who butchered the pseudo language Pig Latin—loved baseball and basketball. At age 9, he became a St. Louis Cardinals fan, which developed into a lifelong obsession.

"It's 1956. I walk around Black Earth in the evening with a radio the size of a lunch box. I tried to hear any station. Then (St. Louis') KMOX 1120 AM comes on, and in the evening, they reached throughout the Midwest. Harry Caray, who I had never heard, was the Cardinals' announcer."

That day, Stan Musial hit a bases-loaded double to win the game, and Caray's enthusiasm appealed to Steve. So, each night, Steve listened to the Cardinals, who were more than 350 miles from Black Earth. Even when the Milwaukee Braves—playing 100 miles east of Black Earth—soared to the top (winning the World Series in 1957), Steve stuck with the Cardinals.

After listening to a few Cardinals' games in 1956, Steve sent a letter to St. Louis. He addressed it this way: "St. Louis Cardinals, Busch Stadium, St. Louis, Missouri."

"No address, no zip code," Steve said. "I wrote, 'I'm Steve Schmitt. I'm 9 years old. I'm a Cardinals' fan....'"

The Cardinals' staff gleefully responded by sending him a dozen four-inch by six-inch black-and-white photos of their most prominent players. Steve was hooked.

Despite having Milwaukee and Chicago teams far closer to his residence, Schmitt remains a longtime Cardinals' season ticket holder—even though the six-hour one-way drive limits him to seeing a few games each year. For years, he also developed friendships with Cardinals' players and coaches. In one Cardinals team photo, with the players wearing red suit jackets, Bob Gibson sported "full quill ostrich black western boots" from Steve's store. In the same picture, then-manager Red Schoendienst also wore shoes from Steve's Black Earth store.

～

SCHMITT PLAYED FOOTBALL, basketball, baseball and, if time allowed, ran track at Black Earth High School. The school consolidated with one in Mazomanie to form Wisconsin Heights High School, where Schmitt was part of the first graduating class in 1965.

His ability to sink baseline baskets, long before the three-point shot, allowed the six-foot-tall player to continue as a member of the Madison Area Technical College basketball team. He earned all-conference honors during his second season and led the league in scoring in 1967; in 1990 he was selected to the school's sports hall of fame.

Schmitt also wanted to play baseball, but the college's athletic department didn't have a team at the time.

With his two-year associate degree in graphic arts, Schmitt worked vigorous manual jobs,

Steve Schmitt as a member of Madison Area Technical College's basketball team, 1966-1967. Photo courtesy Steve Schmitt.

including one at a feed mill where he hauled hundred-pound bags from train cars and, later, moved furniture. He always helped at his father's store, but at age 21 in 1968, he asked to join the business as a shoe salesman. Sales meshed his talkative nature with his ultra competitiveness. He also greeted customers as friends.

"People come *in* for service," Schmitt said. "If I had to knock on doors or use the phone to sell something, it would have been horrible."

Schmitt married high-school girlfriend Julie Skalet in 1968; they settled in Black Earth and had the first of their four daughters the next year. In 1973, Schmitt bought the shoe business and its ample inventory from his father. Later Schmitt changed the name to The Shoe Box and altered the store's focus to shoes. Out went everything, except footwear and products related to it. For 20 years, he also fixed shoes. "I still smell the glue," he said.

The shoe fixation came easily. "In those days, sporting goods stores like Treasure Island and discount places were selling guns and ammo for less than I could buy them for," Schmitt said. "I just kept unloading semi-trucks with shoes."

For 50-plus years, Schmitt sold shoes. And The Shoe Box —located in a sleepy, rural village—thrived over major chains and the online onslaught. It still flourishes with Schmitt's daughters, Emily and Jill, and his son-in-law Paul Schlimgen, handling the business—alongside weekly visits from Steve, who remains the store's owner.

The Shoe Box's massive success was difficult to fathom. Several factors contributed: endless stock on hand; low prices that Schmitt and other salespeople often adjusted because ample sales were needed even if profit margins dipped; astonishing word of mouth; and relentless customer service.

"If someone wants to look at HOKA running shoes, we have sixty styles, not six," Schmitt said. "And everyone likes to tell stories about good experiences. I wanted every experience at The Shoe Box to be good."

Schmitt worked frantically as a salesman for five decades, although The Shoe Box often employed up to seventy or so people, handling part- and full-time work.

"I was up and down three hundred times a day. I laced up three million pairs of shoes," he said. "I put a sign on The Shoe Box door: Call me at home. So, some Thanksgivings and Easters, I'd get a call and go to the store and open it for someone from out of town. I loved it. It didn't bother me at a bit."

Schmitt rarely sat down for lunch. He took minimal breaks. His work schedule some days lasted from 6 a.m. to 9:30 p.m. For many years, Schmitt had up to four "runners" or people who got specific shoes for Schmitt so he could serve multiple customers at once.

From summer 1973 to May 1986, The Shoe Box operated in Black Earth's downtown. Schmitt's store, though, was busting at the seams. Schmitt kept stock everywhere from a vacant grocery store to his parents' basement.

He then built the Shoe Box along two-lane Highway 14 on Black Earth's outskirts, where the store's space skyrocketed and business soared with the new, more visible location. He also bought a former Shell gas station across the street for more storage.

At age 72 on May 18, 2020, during COVID, Schmitt—with troubled knees and hips from constant shoe selling—stepped away from 40- to 60-hour work weeks at The Shoe Box. The store continues to thrive; a random Saturday in August 2024 was filled with more than 100 shoppers and a few dozen green-shirted workers rushing to serve them.

One of the best descriptions of The Shoe Box's success and notoriety came in 2006 from then-Wisconsin State Sen. Dan Kapanke, who owned the Northwoods League's La Crosse Loggers. Kapanke offered this observation of Schmitt and The Shoe Box:

"He makes going to buy a pair of shoes an experience," Kapanke said. "Think about it. He's 40 minutes outside of Madison. Yet many people drive 40 minutes to buy a pair of shoes, so it has become an event. It becomes a destination. That's Steve Schmitt."

How popular is The Shoe Box? Schmitt, modest to a fault, declined to toss out finances. Only when asked about competition from other shoe stores did he finally open up. He said The Shoe Box always held up favorably against a national chain. "Years ago, Famous Footwear was doing well," Schmitt said. "We would take in as much money in one month as they would in a whole freakin' year. That's not an understatement. That's when *they* were at their peak."

AND SCHMITT PLAYED competitive baseball and basketball after work depending on the season. During the baseball season, Schmitt played for two decades in southern Wisconsin's Home Talent League. Also, for 20-plus years after college, Schmitt continued to play basketball. In a basketball travel league that he organized, Schmitt and six teammates played on Sundays, Tuesdays and Thursdays. The basketball team reached 500 wins in their 747 games; twice Schmitt scored 49 points in a single half.

"For basketball, we played 50 to 75 games per year," Schmitt said. "Twelve-minute quarters, and we stopped the clock on every whistle. We played a lot of good teams. A guy could get cut from a pro league on Friday, and he'd play on a Sunday in our league."

The games were physical and exhausting. After two rigorous 12-minute quarters, opponents would describe how good of a workout that was.

"Then I'd say, 'This is halftime,'" Schmitt said, then smiled. "Those were good years."

BASEBALL, in particular, was cemented in Schmitt's blood as he moved away from his playing days. In addition to The Shoe Box, he created Rookies, a sports restaurant and pub in 1998 with a remarkably authentic miniature ball field, best used for Wiffle ball. "I'd see office people playing on their lunch hours. We had doctors from Madison and their staffs playing together," Schmitt said. "And so many kids." The site remains a popular attraction, a roadside stop that will leave families reminiscing about it for years.

Schmitt's love of baseball made his immediate entrance as Madison's sole owner in the Northwoods League understandable. Without notice in January 2001, Schmitt answered a random phone call at The Shoe Box that would pull him back into the sport. It was from Dick Radatz Jr.

"What do you think," Radatz asked Schmitt, "about a summer college baseball team in Madison?"

Schmitt loved the idea, although he knew virtually nothing about the Northwoods League and how they operated.

"I'm all for it," Schmitt responded. "What do you need?"

The Northwoods League's $150,000 franchise fee was within Schmitt's range. Despite his snap decision, Schmitt did not enter the venture blindly. He knew he wanted to keep a summer baseball team in Madison, and he wanted a chance to develop the only suitable baseball diamond with space for expansion: the northside's Warner Park ballpark.

Schmitt was 53 at the time, and his marriage had just ended, although he maintains a good friendship with his ex-wife Julie.

A few months before, in July 2000, The Shoe Box became ground zero for a Madison newspaper's investigation and, later, significant NCAA concern that involved 157 University of Wisconsin athletes receiving discounts on shoes. The school's beloved football team took the biggest hit and received multiple player suspensions.

And, at that unlikely moment, Schmitt bought a baseball team in a market—Madison—that never truly supported one despite more than 100 years of teams trying.

Many, Schmitt said, expected the summer-collegiate team to fail in Madison.

CHAPTER 4
A CITY'S BUMPY BASEBALL PATH

BASEBALL MAINTAINED A ROUGH HISTORY IN MADISON. THE University of Wisconsin's football, hockey and basketball teams dominate the city's sports attention, so the Badger baseball program took a backseat in the UW athletic department—even though the school team developed and played the sport's primitive form only five years after the Civil War's end.

Supported by football profits throughout much of the 20th century, the University of Wisconsin athletic department hit rock bottom in 1989 when revenues generated by the Badgers' cash-cow football program plummeted. The next year, Chancellor Donna Shalala—realizing the sinking football team severely hurt school morale—hired Madison native Pat Richter, a former superstar at Wisconsin in football and, ironically, baseball, as athletic director. Then they landed Notre Dame assistant Barry Alvarez as football coach. (The choices worked extremely well; by 2006, Richter and Alvarez had their statues placed prominently at gigantic Camp Randall Stadium.)

In 1991, however, Wisconsin's athletic department faced a daunting $2.1-million deficit. The school's 1989-90 budget indicated that the baseball team spent $213,360 while earning $1,373 in revenue. Wisconsin's athletic board voted to cut baseball after the sport's 121st season—and the university remains the only Big Ten school without that sport, despite expansions that boosted conference membership to 18 teams.

University of Wisconsin baseball left an intriguing legacy. During their first game in 1870, with archaic period rules (underhanded pitching, no gloves and four outs per inning), Wisconsin's players won their debut by scoring 53 runs. In 1893, Wisconsin earned a forfeit win on the road when opposing fans hurled stones at them after their opponent in Beloit objected to an umpire's call.

By 1975, the University of Wisconsin team was briefly without a home field, and they played a doubleheader against Minnesota at Warner Park, the future Duck Pond. The two games, moved away from campus to attract more Madison residents, drew only 485 fans.

Madison, though, always seemed like an appetizing spot for a minor-league team with a central Midwest location, a growing population and avid sports fans. It never worked out that way.

In 1908, the Madison Senators debuted in the original

Wisconsin-Illinois League, one of 41 minor leagues encompassing 300 teams across the United States. The Wisconsin-Illinois League began life in professional baseball's lowest "D" level. In their second season, the Senators won the eight-team league title, outlasting the Green Bay Bays and the Racine Malted Milks.

By 1915, without producing a notable player, the Senators folded when the league dissolved. Baseball returned to Madison in 1923 when the semi-pro Madison Blues formed. The Blues expanded into a minor league club in 1926, although they jumped across four leagues during their 16-year history, and in the mid-1930s played as few as 17 recorded games in a season.

In 1930, the Blues participated in Wisconsin's first night baseball game when one of many barnstorming teams—this one traveling with floodlights—stopped at Breese Stevens Field. In 1935, the Negro League Pittsburgh Crawfords, with one of baseball's great hitters, Josh Gibson, played two games against the Madison Blues. Gibson, whose lifetime batting average was an astounding .372, helped the Crawfords with his fielding at Breese Stevens Field. He was part of the stadium's first triple play.

And, on Aug. 4, 1938, the Blues attracted 1,800 fans when they booked legendary sprinter and 1936 Olympic Games hero Jesse Owens. After the game, Owens handily beat Blues' center fielder Joe Hady in two sprints, including one around the bases, despite giving Hady sizable head starts. In the third event, Owens suffered a thigh muscle injury on a makeshift 120-meter low hurdle course but won the race.

During their final three seasons, the Blues developed into a bona fide minor-league team, affiliated with the Chicago Cubs and feeding players to the major leagues, before World

War II prompted many minor-league clubs and leagues, including the Blues, to fold. The Blues were part of the Three-I League, a relatively high level organization that originally featured teams from Indiana, Illinois and Iowa (thus the league's name). From 1940-1942, though, the Blues drew a meager 450 fans per game. They were led in hitting during the 1940 and 1941 seasons by infielder Wellington Quinn, nick-named Wimpy after a Popeye cartoon character called J. Wellington Wimpy. (As you recall, Wimpy promised to pay later for a hamburger he consumed today.) What's unusual about Quinn? The six-foot-two infielder and star hitter even-tually landed briefly with the Chicago Cubs—as a pitcher. During spring training, Cubs manager Jimmie Wilson saw Wimpy throw and changed his position.

From 1942 to 1982, an occasional University of Wisconsin baseball game or a Madison-based team's exhibi-tion contest would be noteworthy. An industrial league, with most teams formed among local factories, played night games four times per week in the mid-1940s.

In 1947, the Negro League's Kansas City Monarchs and their star attraction, the legendary Satchel Paige, then 41, pounded a local team called the Industrial All-Stars before 2,903 Madison fans. Paige pitched the first five innings and struck out nine batters, then he hit a sharp single in one of his three at-bats to seal the Monarchs' 14-5 victory.

In 1982, Minor League Baseball returned in the form of the Madison Muskies, a Class-A Midwest League affiliate of the Oakland A's. To a degree, Madison was not ready. Two ownership groups, one from out-of-state and the other local, struggled to cooperate in running the team. The Muskies also did not agree to a lease with the city to play at Warner Park until a few days before opening day.

As a result, the Muskies played their first six home games at Breese Stevens Field, where the former Madison Blues played. Forty years after the Blues' departure, though, Breese Stevens had not been renovated. So, the Muskies were forced to play in a ballpark where the home-run fence along the right-field line was just 240 feet away. The minor leagues rejected a Breese Stevens Field ground rule that anything hit over the short right-field fence counted as a double, not a home run. During those six games at Breese Stevens, 28 home runs—many of them typical fly balls outs to the right-field corner—were hit for round trippers.

Former teacher and political activist Ed Janus helped to bring baseball back to Madison. For the Muskies' first two seasons, Janus shook the city from its baseball slumber and provided an entertaining atmosphere, ranging from a Kazoo Night to crowd chants of "Let's go, Fish!" Janus also hired Hall of Fame pitcher Bob Feller to throw batting practice to fans at $100 per person. Janus was the catcher for the then-64-year-old Feller, who still could throw with some heat. Boosted by rambunctious fans, some using chants heard at University of Wisconsin hockey games, the Muskies received national media attention. (Later, Janus became the co-founder of a hugely successful craft brewery, the Madison-area's Capital Brewery, and, after 2000, he shifted occupations and turned to dairy farming and wrote a notable book on agriculture.) The Muskies drew an average of 1,908 fans in 1983, but that plunged to less than 1,200 by 1990. In 1983, a much-heralded 18-year-old slugger, Jose Canseco, played 34 games for the Muskies, but he hit .159 and three home runs before Oakland shifted him to another minor-league team.

The Muskies barely averted moving from Madison to Kalamazoo, Michigan, in 1990. Then, three years later, they were sold to an ownership group in Grand Rapids, Michigan, where a luxurious new ballpark was built for the new West Michigan Whitecaps.

Madison then became the temporary home of the Class-A Madison Hatters, which drew under 1,000 fans per game before departing for Battle Creek.

After a year without professional baseball, one more team, the Madison Black Wolf, attempted to stir interest. They played in the professional, independent Northern League from 1996 to 2000, and their advantage was that the season wouldn't begin until late May. By then the Northern League was an established entity, with the St. Paul Saints generating national headlines and successful teams in Fargo-Moorhead, Winnipeg and Sioux Falls. But Black Wolf president Bill Terlecky received a rude welcome. In 1996, at his first meeting with then-Madison Parks Department's superintendent Dan Stapay, Terlecky had his enthusiasm crushed.

"Before my butt hits the chair," Terlecky recalled in 2000, "the first words out of his mouth are, 'I don't have a lot of time here.' And I just wanted to say, 'Well, then leave!' I thought, 'If this is how it's going to be, where are we going?'"

Like other Madison teams, the Black Wolf never gained traction. The team's owners lost $1 million, about $200,000 per season. During their tenure, the Black Wolf ownership searched for a new ballpark space, settling at one point on a space near Fish Hatchery and Post roads in the Madison suburb of Fitchburg. The price tag shot up to $9 million to build a new ballpark, quietly ending those discussions.

In September 2000, Terlecky was candid about Madison's struggles to support baseball. Terlecky said the Black Wolf marketed hard to the community, but they did not get much of a response. "There is a lot of blood all over that ballpark," Terlecky said of the team's five-year effort to attract fans.

Terlecky added that professional baseball and Madison did not mix—the Black Wolf, for example, finished last in Northern League attendance by 800 fans per game—and he feared that Warner Park was an inadequate facility.

Still, Terlecky hinted that an amateur summer-collegiate baseball team might work in Madison.

However, he added a warning: "We're telling everyone, don't come in with a grandiose idea that you're going to increase revenues greatly."

∾

Two months before the Black Wolf folded in September 2000, the *Wisconsin State Journal* published an extensive investigation involving dozens of University of Wisconsin athletes who received unannounced discounts at The Shoe Box. That amounted to a serious NCAA violation. In hindsight, it was comical given the current Name, Image and Likeness (NIL) era features some college athletes legally receiving six-figure payments. But a shoe discount 25 years ago became a massive NCAA violation.

The *State Journal*'s mammoth coverage relied, in part, on comments by the friend of a Badger football player and a former Shoe Box employee, both of whom agreed to use their names. But other evidence was supplied by Schmitt himself. In an attempt to show that he reduced prices for everyone, Schmitt gave a few receipts to *State Journal* reporters. The newspaper found some with discounts for Wisconsin players, and one receipt, brightened as he often did to customers, to a football player was plastered across the front page. Wisconsin athletes also received no-interest accounts.

To Schmitt, the media portrayed him as an overzealous college sports booster. There was a rather odder truth: He was an overzealous shoe salesman.

"I've never been a huge Badger fan," Schmitt said. "Teams that came in got treated the same as (Wisconsin) players. I wrote up a bill the same way. It didn't matter who it was; I'd personalize it."

It was important to note that a far lesser-known controversy already put Wisconsin in hot water with the NCAA in 1999, and that affected the NCAA's volatile reaction to The Shoe Box discounts in 2000.

In 1999, the NCAA placed Wisconsin on a two-year probation after an internal audit at the university showed that 77 athletic department staffers and coaches used $200,000 from a booster fund without the school's approval.

So, when The Shoe Box "scandal" hit, the NCAA had more ammunition to strike back. Although 157 athletes in 14 sports were involved with The Shoe Box, Wisconsin's football team, ranked fourth in the nation during preseason, received the most notable punishment. Twenty-six football players had to serve one- to three-game suspensions in the 2000 season's first four games.

On Thursday, Aug. 31, 2000—seven hours before Wisconsin's weeknight opening football game that season— Wisconsin officials learned that the NCAA denied their appeal. So, Wisconsin frantically shuffled its lineup and sat four starters during a 19-7 victory against Western Michigan before 77,843 fans at Camp Randall Stadium. Afterwards,

Alvarez said, "This may be the longest day I've ever had to go through in coaching."

At Warner Park on that same afternoon, the Madison Black Wolf played their second-to-last game ever in front of 284 people. A couple of weeks later, the Black Wolf folded. Then on Dec. 29, 2000, Wisconsin football finished their season beating UCLA in the Sun Bowl.

DURING THE LATE fall 2000 and through early winter 2001, Dick Radatz Jr. gained approval from Madison city officials to bring a Northwoods League team to Warner Park. Radatz negotiated a $250 per game rental fee and promised $10,000 in improvements to the ballpark.

That set the stage for the ambitious league president to hire a young marketing spark plug, Vern Stenman, then combine him with shoe store ace Schmitt.

CHAPTER 5
THE MALLARDS' FIRST HIRE: VERN STENMAN

Vern Stenman in the press box.

SCHMITT KNEW HOW PRECARIOUS OWNING A SPORTS franchise could be. Before buying Madison's Northwoods League team, Schmitt was one of eight owners in a minor-league hockey team called the Madison Kodiaks of the United Hockey League (UHL) in 1999. The Kodiaks lumbered through one season at the 8,000-seat Dane County Veterans Memorial Coliseum, finishing last in attendance with 2,395 fans per game, out of the UHL's 13 teams.

"We kept doing draws from the bank. I had to write checks often," Schmitt said. "We kept our heads up, and I still have good friendships with the other owners, but it was a sad experience."

Schmitt said he learned many lessons from the Kodiaks' failure that helped him build a baseball team. One lesson concerned gaining control of concession revenue. The Kodiaks' arena owner, Dane County, profited from concession sales. The other lesson was that he needed full control of a team.

"I'm not very good at a few things: One is that I don't work well with committees," Schmitt said. "I don't work well with forming a committee to start another committee to make a decision. I hate that. With the Kodiaks, a lot of things got tabled until the next meeting. Then other stuff built up before the next time we met. My theory is 'Let's get it done.'"

During the Kodiaks' season, however, one opponent—the Quad City Mallards—fascinated him. From five combined cities in Illinois and Iowa along the Mississippi River, Quad City, the league's most popular club, brought several busloads of fans for their road game to Madison. Schmitt watched those Quad City fans with fascination. They rang cowbells; they were boisterous; and they were entertaining themselves regardless of what happened on the ice.

"They had more fun than our fans," Schmitt said.

As a result, Schmitt insisted on using the name Mallards when he discussed the Madison baseball team with Radatz—recalling the enthusiasm of the Quad City Mallards fans.

Other name ideas included Madison Moo, Madison Milkmen, Madison Cheese Curds, Madison Holsteins and Madison Milk Pails.

"A lot of dairy. There was no end to it," Schmitt said. "I smiled and said, 'Mallards.'"

About three months before the Madison Mallards debuted, Schmitt drove to Warner Park to see the ballpark. He knew renovations would be significant.

"There was a fence. There were a few picnic tables out in the right-field area," Schmitt said. "The bleachers were horrible." The Mallards staff salvaged a scoreboard but kept it as a manual one with numbers placed on it by hand. The old-school nature of that appealed to them.

Most importantly, Schmitt wanted the ballpark to be known as the Duck Pond. "It seemed kind of childish," Schmitt said, "but the Duck Pond sounds like a fun home that people would remember."

BEFORE APPROACHING Schmitt and assuming he would attract another owner or own the team himself, Radatz began forming a mini staff for the Madison team in January 2001. He pulled 23-year-old Vern Stenman, a sales executive with the NHL's Minnesota Wild, to be the team's marketing director. It was a huge jumpstart.

Despite his youthful age, the eager Stenman spent more than three seasons helping to operate the Northwoods League's St. Cloud River Bats (now the Rox), so he understood summer-collegiate baseball culture and fans. Because he worked full-time for the River Bats during his college's second semester and the summer, he reduced his course load at St. Cloud State University and needed five years to graduate. He didn't regret it, even though he received just $2,500 for a six-month job.

In December 1998, Stenman traveled to New Orleans for the annual professional baseball business convention. Forced to decide between Bourbon Street and paying the hefty convention fees, he snuck into an area where teams posted jobs, and he took 25 to 30 of his resumes and distributed them to many clubs. He received a few offers, but he stuck with St. Cloud.

"It was a cool moment. It was the first moment that I realized I wasn't just wasting my time having fun with this little summer-collegiate baseball team," Stenman said. "I realized that if you knew what you were doing and you proved some success, there was a path to work in sports."

Stenman joined the Minnesota Wild in July 2000, and during his brief time with the club, he helped to create one of the team's initial signature pieces in St. Paul's Xcel Energy Center home: A colorful mini Zamboni, developed by Stenman and his brother, with an organ attached called a "Zamb-organ." While working for the St. Cloud River Bats, Stenman and his family previously had created a small Batmobile out of a golf cart used for promotional purposes, ranging from parades to in-game rides from the bullpen to the mound for relief pitchers.

Still, Stenman learned quickly that ideas seldom flow to fruition in major professional sports. It influenced his Mallards work.

"We want the barrier between a good idea and reality to be really, really small," Stenman said. "We keep our business like this today."

He also wasn't enthusiastic about hockey, and he recalled a Wild staff event where his co-workers skated gleefully on the Xcel Energy Center ice. Stenman, despite being a Minnesota native, never learned to skate in the ice-friendly state.

"Everyone I worked with loved hockey. I felt out of place," Stenman said. "We got to skate on the team's ice. Everyone was so excited; it was hallowed ground for them to skate on NHL ice. That wasn't my thing."

When he heard Radatz planned to have a Northwoods League team in Madison, Stenman contacted him about a job opening. Then Stenman traveled to Madison, where a friend lived. When Stenman arrived on a snowy winter day, he saw a stunning wall of quarry rock surrounding a stadium. He loved the nostalgic exterior—and thought what a fantastic ballpark the new Madison baseball team had.

His friend later corrected him. What Stenman saw was Breese Stevens Field, not Warner Park. They then drove from Madison's downtown to the city's northside, jumped a fence and walked around Warner Park's depressing diamond. Stenman took solace in the fact that Warner Park's ballpark could grow in all directions.

Two months later, Stenman quit the Wild and joined the then-unnamed Madison baseball franchise in the Northwoods League, owned at the time by Radatz. Wild President Tod Leiweke told him, with snark, that he hoped Stenman enjoyed being "a big fish in a small pond." Stenman, however, had baseball in his blood. He said his mom told him that he practically learned to read as a young kid through his subscription to *Baseball America*, which provided detailed news and statistics from the sport's every level. During his junior year at Rocori High School in central Minnesota, he did an elaborate report on legendary baseball marketing maverick Bill Veeck.

Radatz also hired Marc Rardin, 30, as the manager.

Rardin, who also recruited players, had been an assistant coach with both the Northwoods League's Rochester Honkers and Yavapai Junior College in Prescott, Arizona.

Then Anje (pronounced "on-yah") Van Roo joined the team to handle food and beverage sales, a job she did for the Madison Black Wolf. But she soon learned that working for the Mallards meant doing everything, painting to payroll.

Neither Stenman nor Van Roo knew Schmitt personally. Stenman made the connection between Schmitt and Wisconsin's NCAA troubles, which became a national story. At first, Stenman feared that Schmitt was a big-ego Badger booster and not a self-motivated "boot strap" guy like Radatz.

Stenman said Radatz reassured him, "You're going to love this guy."

And Schmitt turned out to be the ultimate "boot strap" owner, who eagerly worked alongside his employees. Stenman and Schmitt did not meet in person until just several weeks before the season.

"I was working late one night. I'm at the ballpark, and it's 9 or so at night," Stenman said. "It's dark out. We worked in two side-by-side trailers. I'm by myself. I see these bright lights. It's this bright yellow Nissan Pathfinder with St. Louis Cardinals' logos. I'm confused. I said, 'Excuse me, what are you doing here?'"

Schmitt responded with a friendly wave.

"I'm Steve," Schmitt said. "I'm the owner of the Mallards."

～

VAN ROO KNEW about Schmitt's tremendous success at The Shoe Box.

"His reputation was very customer focused," Van Roo said. "It was exciting. I knew if he didn't make money in the first season that he wasn't going to say, 'Okay, we need to move the team somewhere else.' Warner Park was a dump compared to other parks. It was what it was. But I knew he would put money into it."

Schmitt did. The city required $10,000 in improvements to the ballpark; Schmitt spent $50,000 in 2001.

When Schmitt arrived for the first time at the team's makeshift office at Warner Park, he found an unwelcome surprise.

"One room had a big architectural drawing of a new ballpark that the Black Wolf were thinking of putting in (suburban) Fitchburg," Schmitt said. "I thought, 'To hell with that.' I have something special with Madison's northside."

Schmitt dressed up Warner Park—now cleverly branded by the team as the Duck Pond—to create a splash for fans. He strung thousands of rope lights, added fake palm trees, bought jumbo figures that wiggle from air pumps and hung disco balls near concession stands. How bad was the park? Before the Mallards debut, trade publication *Ballpark Digest* described it as "an undistinguished civic facility that has no charm, several drawbacks and no compelling reason to draw fans."

In addition to the Mallards' small staff and a few interns, Schmitt brought in workers from The Shoe Box to help paint and to spruce up the ballpark.

"He had what we started calling 'The Sparrow Gang,'" Stenman said. "It was an entourage of Shoe Box workers and friends. We had this support team." Stenman also received almost daily faxes from Schmitt with job lists: painting and cleaning tasks to selecting a song that Schmitt wanted to hear at a certain time of the game.

Schmitt prominently used the slogan "Baseball Like It Oughta Be"—but before the Mallards' first pitch he knew that the sport alone would not draw fans to an amateur summer-collegiate game. "Pure baseball is wonderful—for me," Schmitt said. "You're not going to be successful with just pure baseball. There are just so many fans that are going to keep a scorecard and watch every pitch. There's got to be enter-tainment."

The Duck Pond's only gate was from a left-field entrance adjoining the small clubhouse, so Schmitt and Stenman created what Schmitt said was "to present it like a state fair or a county fair all the way around home plate and up to right field. We would have a spin wheel game for quick prizes. We would launch water balloons from the infield. We would have the (beer-fueled) Duck Blind area."

Madison media avoided the Mallards. The Northwoods League's announcement that Schmitt would be Madison's owner and the team's new name received three sentences, buried inside the sports section, on March 20 in Madison's afternoon newspaper. The city's morning daily newspaper had a season preview for the Mallards focused solely on a former University of Wisconsin football walk-on, Troy Doering, who joined the Mallards.

Schmitt believed firmly that Madison sports reporters had grown weary of another baseball team landing in their city. "That didn't bother me," Schmitt said. "We had to earn cover-age." And Schmitt advertised heavily in the newspapers. A press conference at the Warner Park Community Recreation Center to announce the Mallards name and their logo,

Stenman said, drew almost no one. Still, he added that the team's staffers decided quickly to embrace the Duck Pond.

"We weren't going to bad mouth it," Stenman said. "Instead, we looked at it like a canvas."

Before coming to the Duck Pond each day, Schmitt worked several hours at The Shoe Box. Van Roo said Schmitt appeared like a man on a mission when he arrived. "We had walkie talkies, and when he drove up, we said, 'He's landed.' Whatever you were doing, you had to straighten up."

Schmitt was particular and detail oriented. He installed many Duck Pond signs to assure none were even a fraction of an inch off center.

Thousands of Mallards pocket schedules, though, were printed with a typo in the word "inaugural" on the cover. The mistake was Stenman's—made while he frantically worked to get the Mallards ready for their home opener.

"I heard there's a typo on the pocket schedule," Schmitt told Stenman.

Stenman objected, "I told him, 'There are two ways to spell inaugural.' He said, 'Oh, okay, got it.' And he moved on."

CHAPTER 6
"WHAT THE HELL HAVE I DONE?"

At the Duck Pond's main gate for the Madison Mallards' first-ever home game on June 2, 2001, fans received an individually numbered certificate lavishly thanking them for coming to see "the most gifted college baseball players" who "are here to play, without pay." They also got a free plastic duck-call whistle.

About 1,100 fans attended—with free admission if they lived in Lodi or wore a St. Louis Cardinals cap—to see the Wisconsin Woodchucks shut out the Mallards 4-0. The teams bused back-and-forth, 132 miles one way, after each contest of the four-game series between Wausau and Madison, to avoid the expense of overnight lodging.

But any enthusiasm from Madison fans disappeared after the home opener. Through June and much of July 2001, the Mallards' attendance dipped: Home games tallied just 511, 384 and 259 fans. Van Roo estimated that half of the tickets were complimentary.

Schmitt took the tumbling crowd sizes hard.

"It bothered me. I lost sleep," he said. "I'd bring my

family in and say, 'Look, what we're doing! We're keeping baseball in Madison!' It was embarrassing."

Schmitt—who burned off the hair on his forearms handling the team's open charcoal grill with hot dogs and brats—stepped outside the ballpark during games, so he could count fans from the press box of a high-school football field next door.

"I thought, 'What the hell have I done?' I'd count 274 fans one night," Schmitt said, "then 170 fans the next."

Schmitt invited Jim Gantner, a retired Milwaukee Brewers player but still popular among Brewers fans, to a game. "We both tried to act like we didn't notice that almost no one was there," Schmitt said.

In mid-June, the Mallards guaranteed a victory—or each fan would receive a free ticket to another game. A one-run contest came down to the ninth inning when a rainstorm struck. It wasn't a typical rain delay; winds reached 50 miles per hour, then the lights went out at the Duck Pond. The storm was so severe that fans were told to find shelter in clubhouses or restrooms and not to leave the park. When the game resumed the next day, the Mallards lost 3-2.

On June 20, NCAA investigator Jeff Scott came to Madison to follow up on The Shoe Box situation with the University of Wisconsin. Schmitt spoke to Scott for 90 minutes at the store—where Schmitt took solace in the fact that, with Scott watching, three separate transactions with customers ended with the customer asking him, "What can I have these for?" Unbeknownst to Schmitt or his staff, Scott also attended a Mallards game that night.

What Scott may have seen was a Mallards staff that started bonding while the team played 20 of its 32 home games during June. Postgame gatherings also were cathartic as staff members hung out in the ballpark or the team's cramped offices, located in a double-wide trailer.

One of the staff included Rardin. In late May, Rardin, the Mallards' first manager, left Arizona, where he lived with his wife and their two-month-old son, as he pursued his baseball coaching career. "I'm paying my dues," he said. Anyone questioning his love of the game would be convinced by his son's name: Tyler "Ty" Maddux Rardin. "Ty" was Rardin's shortened name for the infant, and a nod to Ty Cobb. The boy's middle name expressed Rardin's appreciation for pitcher Greg Maddux.

Rardin also used his West Coast contacts to bring a UC-Santa Barbara outfielder named Ryan Spilborghs to the Mallards in late June. Spilborghs would be the Mallards' first-season MVP, and he became the first Mallards player to reach the major leagues, in 2005, where he played seven seasons for the Colorado Rockies.

And Spilborghs was almost booted from the team.

In July, Spilborghs' parents visited Madison and wanted to attend a Milwaukee Brewers game—with their son—at the new Brewers ballpark, Miller Park. Going to the Brewers' game meant Spilborghs would miss the Mallards contest.

"I was furious," Stenman said. "I didn't want to set a precedent that guys could leave whenever they wanted to see another baseball game with their family."

Stenman and Rardin agreed to let the team's players vote whether Spilborghs would stay with the Mallards or be kicked off the team. The charismatic Spilborghs won in a landslide.

Soon after, a team of Northwoods League All-Stars played the touring Team USA, loaded with collegiate stars. Stenman traveled to St. Cloud, for the game, which included the Mallards' low-velocity sidearm pitcher Matt Freisleben.

"Matt was visibly nervous before the game. He throws 78 miles per hour, and he's playing the best amateur players in the country. They had several future big leaguers," Stenman said. To lighten the mood, "I told him, 'Matt, hit your first batter in the back.' We laughed."

Freisleben entered the game...and hit his first batter in the back—not intentionally. He escaped one full inning without allowing a run. The Northwoods League All-Stars used nine pitchers over 10 innings and won 1-0 after an RBI infield single. Team USA proceeded to win their next 12 games on the tour.

"That was a big moment for the league's credibility," Stenman said. "We certainly mentioned that game to attract better players."

Back in Madison, the new Mallards franchise experienced growing pains. Van Roo, with the help of Mallards' staff and a police officer, stopped four young teens who sprinted out of the clubhouse after taking team jerseys and jewelry. All four returned to the Duck Pond to help with clean up after an initial court hearing, and eventually ended becoming part-time employees of the team.

Van Roo—in her mid-30s, a decade older than team staffers who called her "ma'am"—also used bartering deals to help the Mallards, a common practice in minor-league baseball. In one deal, she got a fur coat store to clean the Mallards' mascot outfit in exchange for advertising space. Stenman said Van Roo also taught him to stop using "I" when discussing team plans and say "we" instead to enhance a team-oriented environment. (Stenman said he still uses that advice.)

"Vern was the mastermind," Van Roo said. "He drove me crazy. He was all over the place. But he was a brilliant young man."

Stenman's insistence on an all-you-can-drink for one price, inspired by Radatz' similar venue in Rochester, at the park proved hugely popular with fans, and Schmitt and Stenman kept making sure that the Mallards' name spread.

"Steve did a great job of getting merch in people's hands," said Dennis Degenhardt, a Mallards supporter in their first few years. During the 2001 season, Degenhardt was on his way to the bathroom when he passed Schmitt after the team's regular free T-shirt toss into the crowd. "I said jokingly, 'Damn, I didn't get one,' and I went into the bathroom. Steve thought I was mad. I came out, and he had a really nice Mallards shirt for me. That's Steve."

Relationships formed at the Duck Pond. In July, Stenman met the woman who would become his wife, Kallie, a friend of team sponsors. That same night several Mallards players stayed at the Duck Pond after a game to watch the city's enormous fireworks show while hanging out in the stands. Some players, including Spilborghs, slept on the bleachers that night; Stenman spent the night in a tent set up in center field.

By early August, average attendance inched over 800 per game. That's when a late-season surge of fan support kicked in, proving the Mallards' good-time experience earned word of mouth. Stenman also worked hard to gain the media's support, and he made regular appearances on a morning radio show hosted by one of Madison's most notable and influential broadcasters, John "Sly" Sylvester. The attention boosted the new team, which also used grassroots marketing by having its mascot Maynard walking up and down State Street, a pedestrian-filled eight blocks lined with stores linking the Wisconsin State Capitol building and the University of Wisconsin.

On Friday night, Aug. 3, the Mallards played the season's

last home game against the Brainerd Mighty Gulls. Nearly 2,600 fans, a season high, attended the 2-1 Mallards win. To everyone involved, the big crowd for the finale meant validation and optimism for the team's future. That last game did so well that Van Roo had to scramble to nearby bars to get kegs when the beer supply almost ran out.

Schmitt rejoiced at the crowd size. To this day, the game's box score sits prominently on his desk. Stenman then boasted to reporters that Mallards' season-ending attendance averaged just over 1,000 fans per game.

"It's scary how good this thing can be," Stenman said in August 2001.

Stenman's pronouncement may be from a marketing guy, although he sensed a breakthrough among the city's sports fans. Rardin, who was already set to return for the Mallards' second season, reacted as if he looked into a crystal ball and saw the future. The Mallards, after all, were fourth out of eight Northwoods League teams in 2001 attendance.

Yet, Rardin offered this view after the first season:

"This place is a goldmine," he said. "I've been around a lot of places, and this is a goldmine, from the owner to the front office to the facilities to the town and everything about it."

Hearing Rardin's quote from 2001 for the first time in 2024, Schmitt paused briefly, quiet for a rare moment.

"I love that," he said. "That gives me chills."

CHAPTER 7
A BOBBLEHEAD AIRLIFT

Young fans and their bobbleheads.

NEARLY TWO WEEKS INTO THE 2002 SEASON, THE MALLARDS presented Honker Reduction Night on a Tuesday, giving away one free nose surgery. The team faced the Rochester Honkers, whose nickname, of course, referred to wild geese as opposed to big noses. But Stenman, soon to be the team's general manager, and his small staff thought out of the box to attract attention.

The contest's winner, Schmitt said, "was happier than hell." She bolted up toward the press box to collect the gift certificate for free nose surgery at Facial Cosmetic Center in Middleton, a Madison suburb.

The promotion worked beautifully—and Stenman considered that night as a primary example of how the community came to "expect us to do weird, creative stuff." The Madison media responded to the Honker Reduction Night with enthusiastic coverage. "It was the first time Madison realized we weren't going to be about just baseball," Stenman added. "The Black Wolf was only about baseball. We were about fun."

Cosmetic surgery giveaways by the Mallards were slowed, in part, because physicians declined to participate. "We weren't yelled at by doctors," Stenman said, "but they said, 'That's not really appropriate to offer in a forum like that.'"

Schmitt, Stenman and Rardin cared deeply about the on-field product. Players, especially pitchers, came and went at the whims of their college coaches—one of the known perils for anyone operating a summer-collegiate baseball team. After a few players opted out in May, Rardin tried to restock the team. For example, two players—Texas Tech's Madison Edwards and Oklahoma's Matt Bose, both Midland, Texas, natives—arrived from Dallas at Madison's Dane County Airport and, 40 minutes later, they changed into Mallards uniforms and took batting practice. Then they played immediately in the team's home opener.

A few weeks into the season, Rardin, the manager, departed unexpectedly. Seeking another advancement up the baseball ranks, Rardin left to become pitching coach at Lamar Community College in Lamar, Colorado.

BEFORE THE 2002 SEASON, the Mallards searched for a radio station to broadcast Mallards games. Commercial radio stations immediately rejected them. The Mallards eventually landed on student-run WSUM-FM, the University of Wisconsin's nonprofit station. The announcers were novices, and between innings, a disc jockey played raucous college rock in the studio because they did not air commercials.

Mallards 2002 promotions, meanwhile, included Summertime St. Pat's Day with green bases, baselines and uniforms, which was "essentially a T-shirt," Stenman said, "something we wouldn't use today."

On Aug. 12, 2002, the Mallards offered the first of the team's 110-plus bobblehead promotion giveaways. It featured, as did many bobbleheads in the team's first few seasons, Mallards mascot Maynard. "At that time, it wasn't common to offer bobbleheads. We did a T-shirt to commemorate it. From 2002 to 2012, bobbleheads meant a big crowd," Stenman said. "We saw bobbleheads coming as a trend. For us, it became a storytelling piece." As a result, bobbleheads eventually featured everyone from the team's mohawk-haired vendor to the late Madison native and comic actor Chris Farley to then-presidential candidates Barack Obama and Mitt Romney in Mallards jerseys.

It was a wild 2002 season. The Mallards' popular public address announcer, Rich Reynolds, playfully taunted the Mankato MoonDogs during a game over the Duck Pond's speakers. Reynolds humorously poked at opposing teams all season, but Reynolds savored the MoonDogs' miscues and began crowd chants of "left, right" as MoonDogs' players returned to the dugout after striking out. Upset by the comments, Mankato's Rusty McClain, who was managing the MoonDogs in their first season, rushed to the press box and threatened him physically, Reynolds said. In late July, two days after the Mallards lost 14-13 to the St. Cloud River Bats, Northwoods League officials stepped in regarding Reynolds' in-game comments. They fined Reynolds $100 for taunting St. Cloud players.

"The actual reason for the fine was 'creating a hostile environment towards the visiting team,'" Reynolds said. Rattled by his previous confrontation with the Mankato manager, Reynolds said that he already "changed tactics but not antics. I would meet with the visiting manager and team before games to let them know what I did was all for fun and for the fans' enjoyment. That seemed to quell future incidents, and the teams rarely responded to heckling from our fans. Those early days of the Mallards were wild times."

Schmitt paid Reynolds' fine to the league, which Reynolds called a "gracious" gesture because "money was tight for me in those days."

The eight-team Northwoods League ended 2002 drawing an average of 1,365 fans, up from 1,082 in 2001. The Mallards' record was a dismal 24-40—the first of only two seasons in their history with a sub-.500 record—but they drew an impressive 1,846 per game. That tally began to jump annually.

$\sim$

BEFORE THE 2003 SEASON, the Mallards introduced the renovated Great Dane Duck Blind party deck, offering more than 500 fans with the option—and it was embraced quickly —of all-you-can-drink beer. Mallards fans were thirsty.

It was hard to imagine that in the second largest city of America's heaviest drinking state per capita the Mallards could not initially land a beer sponsorship. "In the early 2000s, Wisconsin was a Miller (beer) state," Stenman said. But his meetings, at the time, with Miller management "were not pleasant" to the upstart baseball team.

In 2002, a local brew pub, Great Dane, partnered with the Mallards, and the result meant the team offered 17 different craft beers. Budweiser followed. Although fans could drink anywhere in the Duck Pond, Stenman created a restricted party zone in the right field for the Duck Blind. That allowed the Mallards to appeal to the raucous party crowd while maintaining a growing reputation as family friendly.

During the last 15 years, Madison has always earned a spot as one of the nation's booze-friendly cities, whether the list came from *Men's Health* magazine or the website *24/7 Wall Street*. It also did not matter how researchers measured consumption; Madisonians, like countless residents of Wisconsin, consumed plenty of alcohol and proudly boasted that consumption as part of their culture. (In July 2023, one prominent ranking put Madison at fourth as the nation's heaviest drinking city. Places with Northwoods League teams, incidentally, occupied seven of the country's top 12 most boozy places on that list.)

"It hasn't been problematic," Stenman said. "We expanded our staff to add several off-duty police officers working for us. Every few years, we got asked, 'Is this a good idea? Is this safe?' We were always able to respond that it was."

The Mallards were quick to lighten the Duck Blind's buzz. They hired kitchen staff to tell them how to guarantee that all-you-can-eat food would be available with little wait time. The response? Build a kitchen in right field. The Mallards did it.

How popular was the Duck Blind? At 11:30 on a Friday night in the 2004 season, the Mallards placed 100 additional Duck Blind tickets on their website for the next evening's game. By early Saturday morning, every ticket was sold.

For many years after most games, about 30 to 40 cars remained in the Duck Pond's parking lot overnight. Stenman pointed to that as an example how Mallards attendees planned ahead, using other options home if they had been drinking too much in the Duck Blind.

Who took the brunt of the Duck Blind's popularity? Opposing right fielders, with the Mallards' most boisterous fans easily within ear shot.

BEFORE THE 2003 SEASON, the Mallards hired Darrell Handelsman, who managed the Waterloo Bucks to the North-woods League title in 2002. With Waterloo one year, Handelsman worked nine months as a waiter, then managed the Bucks. With the Mallards, he had a full-time job that included sales, marketing and public relations.

As a manager, Handelsman was known for pushing an upbeat game, featuring plenty of stolen bases and hustling for the extra base. That style of play was designed to put pressure on opposing pitchers, but it also had the side benefit of exciting fans.

Former Milwaukee Brewers star Jim Gantner declined the Mallards managerial job. (A few years later, Gantner inquired about managing the Mallards, but the position was filled; Gantner then coached the Wisconsin Woodchucks for two seasons.) Handelsman and the Mallards staff brought in an almost entirely new player roster.

At the same time, the Mallards enjoyed a lengthy period of positive publicity and community goodwill.

Media outlets gave extensive coverage to the team's preseason auditions to fill a vital position: mascot Maynard. Timothy Bartelt, a suburban Madison native who also planned to work in a chocolate factory during the summer, won the competition after he jumped on the judges' wobbly table, where Schmitt, Stenman and other team staff sat. Then Bartelt, in full costume, climbed atop the third-base dugout to dance to "Macarena." Bartelt finished with a full circle spin despite the bulky costume.

New Madison mayor Dave Cieslewicz threw out the first pitch at the Mallards home opener, and ex-Milwaukee Braves' star Johnny Logan, a four-time all-star shortstop and Schmitt's friend, eagerly continued to make appearances at the Mallards home openers. More than 5,600 fans—at the time, a national summer-collegiate record—attended the Wednesday night game.

In 2003, the Northwoods League also kept their teams playing and playing. The Mallards' relentless schedule, for instance, included 42 straight games from June 3 to July 14 without a day off. Travel was brutal. Early in the season, the Mallards played a night game in Rochester, then traveled nearly 600 miles, more than 10 hours by bus, to play the next evening in Thunder Bay, Ontario, Canada.

During a mid-June road trip to La Crosse, the Mallards stayed at the Best Western Midway, less than a mile from Copeland Park, home of the La Crosse Loggers. Trouble was, the team received eight free hotel rooms, causing four players to bunch in one cramped room. As soon as players arrived at their hotel, they often called the front desk to request extra cots, blankets and pillows.

Six-foot-nine pitcher Andy Sigerich was one of the Mallards in 2003. He joined the team before his second year at the University of Illinois in Champaign. Like every Mallard, playing professional baseball was his goal. A suburban Chicago native, Sigerich opted for college baseball after the Milwaukee Brewers picked him in the 31st round when he finished high school. Low round picks, though, often faced longshot odds to the big leagues, and they lost their chance at bonus signing money when they were available to be drafted again after their junior year in college.

So, Sigerich found himself as a Mallard in a confined La Crosse hotel room in June 2003.

"I might just sleep on the floor," he said at the time. "A lot of the places we stay, the carpet is softer than the beds anyway."

ON JULY 3, 2003, the Mallards drew a big crowd for their second bobblehead giveaway, featuring Maynard at bat. More than 1,500 boxed bobbleheads were made in China and imported to Los Angeles. The Mallards order was on its way to Madison by truck. Then the truck broke down in North Platte, Nebraska, 718 miles from the Duck Pond. By noon that day, it seemed like the splashy promotion was doomed. Then the Mallards staff talked to a local pilot, who connected them with a private aviation company.

"We hired a plane to fly these bobbleheads from North Platte to Madison," Stenman said.

The plane arrived a few miles from the Duck Pond about 35 minutes before game time. The Mallards workers already had passed out coupons to receive the bobblehead on another day. At 6:30 p.m., though, Stenman and five Mallards interns went to the airport and loaded boxes filled with bobbleheads into several cars—then returned to the Duck Pond. After the game started, the public address announcer proclaimed, "We have the bobbleheads!"

Stenman felt proud about the extreme lengths that the Mallards went to fulfill the game's promotion.

"We delivered," Stenman said. "We set that standard with our staff to take care of our fans."

THE MALLARDS HOSTED the 2003 Northwoods League All-Star Game for the second straight year with good results. At the 2002 All-Star event, the Duck Pond's distant home-run fences—360 feet to the left- and right-field corners—were too much for the league's best sluggers. The first six batters failed to hit anything longer than what would have been hard singles or, at best, a double. Stenman feared the worst: He thought, "Maybe get a tape measure out there and check for the longest hit?" Finally, two Mallards, Charlie Babineaux and Jaime Martinez, each hit homers—and that was enough to create an extra round and an eventual winner.

In 2003, the Duck Pond's expanded Duck Blind caused the right-field corner fence to be pushed in by 50 feet. That allowed for several homers in the pregame Home Run Derby. During the actual All-Star Game, Wisconsin Woodchucks infielder Ben Zobrist belted a three-run double. (Thirteen years later, Zobrist was the World Series MVP, significantly helping to end the Chicago Cubs' 108-year streak without a championship.)

The All-Star Game day was exhausting for everyone. Former Los Angeles Dodgers star and coach Tommy Davis, another of Schmitt's friends, gave a keynote speech at the All-Star luncheon. Scouts then watched the Northwoods League players take batting and fielding practice—and timed each player running a 60-yard dash. The Home Run Derby and All-Star Game followed. And during the day, Dick Radatz also offered a glowing update on the Northwoods League and potential expansion.

"It used to take us two years to get a call about a franchise," Radatz said. "Now we literally get one each week."

After the All-Star festivities, at 2 a.m., the many teams' young officials, most in their twenties, took batting practice in the Duck Pond. Stenman had been given a T-shirt launcher during the event and someone wondered if they could put a baseball in it and try to hit those pitches. Before anyone stepped to the plate, they tested it; and the T-shirt launcher fired a 100-plus-mph fast ball with the erratic movement of a knuckleball.

"The ball exploded out of this launcher," Stenman said. "It didn't spin, but it cut all over the place. It would have been terribly dangerous to bat against." So, the young team execs launched balls from home plate far over the scoreboard—and sent a wood bat rocketing into the outfield. The night calmed down a bit after a friendly visit from a Madison Police officer reminding the group to turn off the loud music played from the PA system.

SCHMITT'S CONNECTIONS helped to attract many former baseball stars to make appearances and to sign autographs at Mallards games. Some players were many years removed from stardom, including veteran home-run hitter Roy Sievers (a 1950s star in Washington and St. Louis over a 17-year career), and others were Hall of Famers, such as Gaylord Perry. The latter charged $2 per autograph in a 2002 Mallards guest stint, but he signed everything, including Vaseline jars, containing one of the substances that got Perry in trouble for doctoring baseballs during his career.

Former Milwaukee Brewers players always drew welcoming crowds at Mallards games. "Stormin'" Gorman Thomas was one of them. But his July 19, 2003 appearance showcased "Grumpy" Gorman. Before the Mallards game, his signatures were scattershot. He used a Sharpie on baseballs and a pen on pictures; baseball players learned immediately it was the other way around. A Brewers favorite during his 11 years with the team from 1973-1983, Thomas was paid in full in advance.

"He was miserable, terrible," Stenman said. "He clearly didn't want to be there."

After signing some autographs, Thomas threw out the first pitch, then rushed toward the front gate to leave while 200 more fans stood in line for his autograph. Intern Conor Caloia —a University of Wisconsin student, who would become the team's chief operating officer—raced after Thomas in the parking lot, but the ex-Brewer, cigarette in his mouth, did not return.

"I kept saying, 'Mr. Thomas, Mr. Thomas, Mr.

Thomas…'" Caloia said. "I followed him, 'Can you please come back?' The answer was no."

Mallards officials learned their lesson about special guests: Pay half upfront, then pay the rest after their completed appearance. (Years later, the Mallards were contacted about using Gorman Thomas' new barbeque sauce called "Stormin' Sauce"; they quickly declined.)

Other athletes and celebrities understood the guest gig's role when making these paid appearances. It was easy money with the bonus of an ego boost. Some notables were fantastic. Stenman mentioned multiple Mallards guest promotion stops by Paul Molitor, who recalled remarkable details about a Wisconsin minor-league park that he played in for only a three-game series decades before. "It wasn't about the paycheck for the biggest stars, Molitor especially," Stenman said. "He got paid fairly. But I sensed he felt an obligation to the state of Wisconsin because of his time with the Milwaukee Brewers to do it. He was outstanding with the fans."

Former Minnesota Twins star Harmon Killebrew, a last-minute substitute for "Goose" Gossage, was another stellar special guest. Killebrew's autograph line extended far from his table. Stenman anxiously watched the Hall of Fame slugger sign his autograph neatly but slowly when he approached Killebrew.

"We're glad you're here," Stenman told Killebrew. "Is there any chance you can speed your signatures up because there's almost 1,000 people in line?"

Killebrew, not angry but stern, looked at Stenman.

"These people are patient enough to meet and get my autograph," Killebrew said, "so I'm going to make sure they get a good autograph."

Years later, Stenman remembered the story. "He couldn't

have been nicer about it. Most of these guys knock out their autograph pretty quickly. Killebrew didn't, not even a little bit. Many Hall of Famers and superstar players also are really good people."

~

In 2003, the Mallards kept breaking their single-game attendance record, which also counted as the most popular summer-collegiate game ever. On July 12, 2003, a record 5,776 fans showed up at the Duck Pond. One week later, the Mallards topped that and attracted 6,018 fans. And the season wasn't finished until Aug. 7, 2003, when they drew 7,491 for their regular-season finale on a Thursday night.

For the season, the Mallards sold 136,751 tickets—20,000 more than four other teams combined in the 10-member Northwoods League. The Mallards' 4,411 per game attendance easily doubled what the highly touted minor-league Madison Muskies drew in 1983, their most popular season.

It was tough on the Mallards staff: four full timers, including the head coach, and four interns. Caloia, who was 20 and about to enter his senior year at Wisconsin, recalled that 8:30 a.m. to midnight days were fairly common. He chose the Mallards internship over one with the United States Bobsled and Skeleton Federation in Lake Placid, New York, because he figured he would have time to enjoy his University of Wisconsin fraternity's lakeside house while with the Mallards. Instead, he worked "around the clock."

"My dad asked, 'What are you doing?' It was intense and the pay was $1,000 for the summer," Caloia said. "But it was the best thing I ever did. It built my work ethic. I learned the business. I was the public relations intern, but for the first three innings of every game, I was at a grill behind home plate with (owner) Steve (Schmitt) and we would turn hot dogs. Then I moved kegs of beer around the stadium and did security. When the game ended, I wrote a game story without watching the game. I dissected the box score to write the game story."

Even fireworks were launched by Stenman and Caloia—until one mishap.

During a 2003 weekday afternoon game with many kids in attendance, the Mallards opted to shoot fireworks during the National Anthem. Stenman lit some fireworks that shot out—not up.

"It knocked us off this four-foot-wide by six-foot-high platform," Caloia said. "I had burn holes in my shirt and pants. I couldn't hear in my left ear. I took my walkie talkie and said, 'I quit!'"

Fifteen minutes later, Caloia returned to work, but the Mallards hired a fireworks company to handle their displays. Caloia said his hearing in his left ear returned a few days later.

Other teams—and sports business officials—around the country noticed the Mallards success, and for-profit summer-collegiate leagues continued to grow. The Mallards had set the bar higher than anyone imagined—and they would raise it higher.

"The amazing factor in Madison is that there was a negative history behind baseball," said La Crosse Loggers general manager Chris Goodell. "You look across the nation, when there's been a failed attempt, some negative history, that's awful hard to rebound from and to capitalize on. They have, and in a big way."

Schmitt kept watch on all aspects of the Duck Pond's appearance. Rather than pocket Mallards profits, Schmitt—

whose success at The Shoe Box made him financially secure —continued to enhance the Mallards' home.

In 2002, Schmitt moved from Black Earth, where he was a five-minute drive from his massive shoe store, to Stoughton, a Madison suburb and a 50-minute drive to The Shoe Box. He did not listen to the radio or to music on his countless drives to the store. "I'm fascinated with thinking," he said. "I just relax. I think about business and life."

In 2003, Schmitt owned the area's most popular team… without the nickname Badgers. He loved the Mallards. Asked whether the Mallards' bubble could burst, Schmitt winced, then declared, "I'm not too sure about anything, but I would never let that happen."

In the Mallards office at that time, Stenman and Mallards staff considered the same challenge.

"We thought, 'Next year's gonna be the best year,'" Stenman said. "That was our rallying cry."

Through May 2020, Schmitt also maintained his relentless work at The Shoe Box, where he worked so hard that he wore out a pair of Red Wing Irish Setter boots almost monthly.

The store's décor featured hundreds of shoes on display mixed with sports memorabilia. Like the Duck Pond, it was gaudy and mesmerizing. Schmitt also put autographed photos, family pictures, area high-school team banners and Mallards team posters everywhere. There was so much memorabilia and so many good-will plaques—given to Schmitt for annual support of Easter Seals events to a congressman's proclamation touting Schmitt's "service in the field of education"—the store had no empty space on its walls. Pull a cowboy boot off a store shelf in one store area, for instance, and the customer could see a vintage autographed photo of legendary pitcher Bob Feller. It was—and remains—a quirky museum planted inside a mammoth shoe store.

The bathroom walls are covered with autographed sports cards behind a plastic shield. There is no rhyme or reason to the cards' placement; one bunch of six cards features basketball star Gail Goodrich, baseball's Dave Kingman, San Francisco Giants outfielder Ted Wood, NHL winger Brian Propp, early 1950 women's baseball player Joan Berger and football running back Stump Mitchell.

"A lot of these (items) are gifts," Schmitt said. "[Customers] might bring me something that they had or their uncle had. It spans back to the '80s.

"Then a high-school coach would bring in a helmet and a rival school coach would see it at the store and say, 'I'm bringing you one of ours.'"

CHAPTER 8
"WITH SPORTS TEAMS, THERE IS CONFLICT"

BEFORE THE 2004 SEASON STARTED, HANDELSMAN—WHILE still managing the Mallards—explored joining his father, Lew, in Fayetteville, North Carolina, with the Coastal Plain League's Fayetteville SwampDogs. Lew was about to buy the team, which played out of decrepit J.P. Riddle Stadium, a former MiLB ballpark that matched Warner Park in condition and status. The Handelsman family wanted Stenman to operate the team and offered him part ownership. They planned to recreate the Mallards magic in Fayetteville.

Stenman, then 26, was the Northwoods League's reigning executive of the year. He was a significant factor in the Mallards' popularity, and he traveled to Fayetteville and toured the ballpark.

"I put serious thought to it," said Stenman. "Coming to Madison (in February 2001), I thought I was only going to be here a couple of years then move on and do something else in sports. Initially, I saw (the Mallards) as a stepping stone for me."

Former Mallard Ryan Rogowski, league MVP in 2005.

With the 2004 Mallards season nearing, Stenman declined the Fayetteville job offer, in part, because his older brother, who was in the military, painted a bleak picture of Fayet-teville, home to Fort Bragg. Shortly after, other opportunities popped up for Stenman with minor-league teams, and he extensively considered a Colorado summer-collegiate league's interest in having him generate expansion.

Schmitt stepped in after Stenman turned down the Fayet-teville job. He acknowledged Stenman's imperative work to the Mallards' growth, and their working relationship cemented the team's popular success for more than two decades.

"I know other sports team owners across the country, and I probably wouldn't have lasted as long with them," Stenman said. "I'm pretty independent. I want to do what I want to do, and other traditional sports team owners might have said, 'Wait another year to build that.' Or 'Why don't you do it this way?'"

He continued: "Steve has always treated me fairly. He's open about whatever the heck is bothering him, but I've never come to Steve with an idea, and he says, 'That's terrible.' There's trust there."

And Schmitt received honesty in return.

One time, Schmitt suggested to Stenman that they add a second Northwoods League team in Madison's Duck Pond—noting it would be "just like when the St. Louis Cardinals and the St. Louis Browns shared Sportsman's Park" from 1920 to 1953.

Schmitt outlined his plan: "'Let's have a (home) game *every* night. Bring in another home team here. If the Mallards are on the road, they could play. Let's have 72 home games a year!' I was serious."

Knowing the amount of work, marketing and expenses to have one successful baseball team, Stenman listened to the proposal and gently mentioned the extreme difficulties—then he could not avoid Schmitt's baseball enthusiasm before explaining the impossibility. (Still, in 2024, Stenman and Schmitt launched a for-profit collegiate women's summer softball team, the Madison Night Mares, adding 21 home games to the Duck Pond's slate.)

Schmitt admired Stenman, and, in 2005, Schmitt said he realized quickly during the Mallards' first season how good Stenman was when he joined late-night discussions about how to draw fans.

Schmitt recalled: "I said, 'This is the guy. He's gotta be here next year and the following year.' He was a good baseball guy, and you could see that right away. He loved the game, and he loved the fans just like I do."

FOUR MALLARDS PLAYERS in 2004 showed how unique the roster was each season, and one of this quartet never made it to Madison.

Handelsman brought in third baseman Chris Frk, a University of Illinois player who received a fifth year in college after redshirting. Frk played three seasons with the Waterloo Bucks and, as a Mallard in 2004, he broke the record for most games (187) played in the Northwoods League. He proceeded to finish his Northwoods League career by appearing in 227 games, which remains a league record, and contributed to what would become one of the Mallards' most successful seasons on the field.

Also in 2004, outfielder Matt Musser, a Madison native, played with the Mallards for three weeks, then left for required service duty at the Air Force Academy. The roster constantly rotated (not unusual any season), and the Mallards landed University of Texas reliever Kyle Yates, a member of the Longhorns' NCAA College World Series runner-up. Before the college tournament ended, though, Yates had been drafted in the 13th round by the Toronto Blue Jays, so he skipped the Mallards and began a five-year professional career. Another player from a small Minnesota college departed the Mallards roster after going hitless in 24 at bats.

Frk, however, stayed with the Mallards throughout the eventful season—and marveled at playing in that season's game when a record-setting 10,061 fans packed into the Duck Pond. He was never drafted into the major leagues, although he earned All-Big Ten honors. In early fall 2008—28 months after graduating from Illinois while working in finance in Chicago—Frk was diagnosed with testicular cancer. At one point during extensive chemotherapy, Frk had rapid weight loss of 20 pounds. Later, as a cancer survivor, Frk became director for a financial advisor firm in Charlotte, North Carolina. He also served as a cancer patient advocate: Since 2009, he has been an active board member for the 24 Foundation, which supports cancer treatment and research.

Replacing a chain-link fence, the Mallards' new green front gate, with an arch featuring the team's logo, greeted fans when the 2004 season started. The team added new lights, much-needed concession expansion and new business offices that also served as ticket booths. The business offices remained from the 1980s Madison Muskies, but the team's emphasis on fans meant the Mallards' nice exterior masked the offices' bland interior. (To this day, the offices are relatively small, and the space feels a bit cramped. During a meeting in fall 2023, rain leaked through the roof and poured across Stenman's desk.) Instead, in 2004, Mallards profits went toward a two-story left-field seating area, an improved bullpen and the Duck Pond's area for children.

And fans kept coming in droves. The Mallards also won their first Northwoods League title, beating the Duluth Huskies 4-3 at the Duck Pond in 11 innings. Frk, playing in his final Northwoods League game, scored the Mallards' third run that forced extra innings. Then, playoff MVP Doug Beck notched the winning run when the Huskies tossed a sacrifice bunt into the outfield.

Behind the scenes, though, Handelsman and Stenman did not talk to each other for the season's last seven weeks. The rift was kept quiet.

"So many times with sports teams, there is conflict," said Stenman, who said his decision not to follow Handelsman to Fayetteville was only one incident that led to their impasse. And winning the title eased matters. (In 2014, Schmitt and Stenman hired Handelsman to manage their Northwoods League team in Green Bay.)

The Mallards' championship team featured four Mallards outfielders who would be drafted by major-league teams— Illinois' Ryan Rogowski, St. John University's Greg Thomson, Xavier's Jay Johnson and Fort Hays State's Jeff Bieker. That talent was matched by enthusiasm from the fans: one supporter, for instance, had a coaster-sized Mallards logo tattoo placed permanently on his bicep. The Mallards also were a desired spot for other college players seeking scouts' attention. At 2 a.m. on the night that Mallards won the title, Stenman glanced at his email: Three players already contacted him about joining the team in 2005.

TEN DAYS after sealing the 2004 title, the Duck Pond became home to a Bob Dylan and Willie Nelson concert, drawing a sellout crowd of nearly 15,000 people. The concert was booked by iconic promoter Ken Adamany—who helped launch Cheap Trick to stardom and brought Jimi Hendrix and many other stars to Madison—and negotiated the show through the city.

The savvy Adamany then hired the Mallards staff to handle all concessions. With cash-only sales, Adamany told the Mallards to have lines for beer tokens separate from beer stands.

During the pre-concert set up, Dylan's crew concentrated on the icon's privacy by building a runway that extended from his tour bus to the stage. Willie brought another fear: Madison Police expressed concerns that biker gangs were coming to see Willie perform. That never happened.

At 9:30 p.m., Dylan finished his headlining set and, five minutes later, it started raining. Stenman and Caloia were "novices for this type of event," Stenman said. But the rain prompted everyone to move quickly out of the Duck Pond, eliminating another fear that fans wouldn't leave.

Then Stenman, Caloia and others hand counted $160,000 cash from beer sales. The money was placed in the Mallards' safe after they gave $40,000 to Adamany that night.

"We had cardboard boxes full of cash," Stenman said. "Conor and I got in my Jeep Wrangler with the top open and at 10 a.m. we drove to the bank. We had $120,000 in cash! It felt very vulnerable. The deal was good for the promoter. I'm not sure we made much after we paid all of our expenses, but it was a highlight of my career. I'm a big Dylan and Willie fan."

WITHIN WEEKS of the season's end, Handelsman announced that he was leaving to manage and to be director of operations for the Fayetteville SwampDogs, by then owned by his father.

Handelsman led Fayetteville for the next nine seasons, including an appearance in the league's championship series during his last year. The 2012 Fayetteville season was a hardship for Handelsman. After recovering from a heart attack, he was one of four people burned in a gas explosion at a Swamp-Dogs' concession stand a few weeks before the season's start. Handelsman burned his legs, arms and part of his face and spent several weeks in a Chapel Hill hospital's burn unit to heal. "It took me a week before I wanted to look in the mirror," he said. "It was scary." He still returned to manage the team on July 3.

His father, Lew, folded the team in 2019 when he could not reach an agreement with the technical college that became the owner of the SwampDogs' home park.

AFTER THE 2004 SEASON, the Mallards adjusted their ticketing. They started selling 10-ticket books encouraging fans to get a reserved seat in advance. Nearly 3,500 of these ticket books sold before the 2005 season. Mallards staffers were amused that some people assumed working for the team was only a summer job—as if the huge crowds just magically show up.

"We were competing with ourselves, and we kept expanding the fan experience," Stenman said. "We never thought we would draw 6,000 fans per night—or have more than 10,000 for one game. We didn't think that was possible."

The Duck Blind continued to be a popular attraction. The cost held at $27 for unlimited food, beer and soda. But the Mallards also held up to 50 tickets on game day for the Duck Blind that cost $20.

"We don't want to get too far from our roots," Stenman said in 2005. "We've been based on being affordable and being creative, not necessarily going the typical route. The typical route would have been to take that exact area and make it into a suite and sell it for premium dollars."

Caloia, the team's assistant general manager in 2005 and 2006, said the Duck Blind went from "a little party to a big party so fast."

How much the Mallards' notoriety increased was most evident when they opened their fifth season at the Duck Pond. Five people threw out the first pitch, including Wisconsin Gov. Jim Doyle. He followed Madison Mayor Dave Cieslewicz, local TV sports anchor Jay Wilson, a sponsor's son, and Mallards supporter and ex-Milwaukee Braves shortstop Johnny Logan.

With a few returnees from the 2004 championship team, the 2005 Mallards had a bit more perspective about the lengthy road trips and their desire to become professionals than other players. At one point, the schedule put them on the road in seven straight different cities. While away, they clinched the Northwoods League's South Division first-half title, guaranteeing a playoff berth, but they had played 17 days in a row without a home game.

Third baseman Kelly Sweppenhiser, who attended

Virginia Military Institute and would be drafted by Toronto
Blue Jays in 2006, said after the exhausting road trip that it
helped players learn what life is like in the minor leagues.

"You figure out really how much you love this game,"
Sweppenhiser said, "and how bad you want to play at the next
level."

When the Mallards returned from that road trip, more than
7,200 fans cheered at the Duck Pond as they crushed La
Crosse, 13-1.

In 2005, the Mallards began their decade-plus relationship
with David "The Bullet" Smith, a human cannonball
performer. "We were pushing the circus-feel to the ballpark,"
Stenman said. He found Smith by typing "human cannonball"
in an online search. Smith was the perfect pick. His father had
been a long-time human cannonball, and David was well-
established at the craft. The Mallards are considered to be the
first baseball team to ever feature a human cannonball show,
and Smith had extended the promotion to hundreds of MLB
and MiLB ballparks.

For his first Mallards appearance, the team kept his act
quiet. During postgame fireworks, they incorporated Smith
into the show by launching him from centerfield to a small net
at home plate. "It was a nod to Bill Veeck," said Stenman,
referring to the master baseball executive. "He believed in not
always telling people what was going to happen, then do
something memorable so they didn't miss the next game."

By 2005, Stenman became a media favorite; and, two
years later, Madison's popular alternative weekly newspaper
Isthmus dubbed him "Mr. Mallard" in a cover story. Schmitt

maintained control of the Mallards, but Stenman handled operations and just about anything: solving a problem with the inflatable air castle; helping to pour beer, if needed, in the Duck Blind; handling the microphone in the stands for name-that-tune quizzes; and dealing with a disruptive fan during miniature bat night. He made 6 a.m. appearances on local TV newscasts, then stayed at the Duck Pond until 1 a.m.

"He's always going a hundred miles an hour," said second-year Mallards reliever Matt Petty.

Third-year Mallards player Mike Rohde added, "He's like a hummingbird flying around. He treats everything kind of like the world's on fire and he's got to put out the fire. He's awesome. Just a ball of energy."

In fall 2005, Stenman met with an architect to discuss major changes remodeling to the Duck Pond. Stenman's goal? Guarantee 7,500 fans have a nice view of the game.

Less than a minute after walking on the field, the architect arrived at the solution:

Turn the ballpark orientation around 180 degrees, with the infield shifting to center. The Mallards staff loved the idea and wanted to do it.

CHAPTER 9
THE GARY COLEMAN LESSON

Umpire Jack Herbert and Gary Coleman square off.

WHILE THE MALLARDS DEVELOPED A $4 MILLION RENOVATION plan in 2006 for the Duck Pond—with the ballpark and field orientation spun the opposite direction—Mallards media coverage spotlighted Schmitt's commitment to making the team thrive.

Before the 2006 home opener, Schmitt, then 59, received a glowing profile in the *Wisconsin State Journal*. The profile was notable for reflection by Wisconsin's associate athletic director Vince Sweeney, one of the few remaining school officials who worked there when The Shoe Box incident happened. Sweeney praised the Mallards and their success.

"It's a really a treat to watch," Sweeney said. "The whole Mallards operation has been a very positive boon to the landscape in Madison. We're very proud of them. From being in the athletics business, to see what they're doing, it's pretty cool."

Sweeney continued to stress that Wisconsin fans did not hold a grudge against Schmitt.

"I don't think there was ever any malice or feeling of ill will. I think most people understand we needed to be responsible for our own actions. It was our actions that led to probation. I don't think our fans took it out on Steve Schmitt. I hope they didn't."

The story ended with Schmitt expecting the Mallards to expand their enormous popularity after their first five seasons. "I still think we've got a base hit," Schmitt said, "and we're chugging for second base."

IN JUNE 2006, the Mallards lost 10 of 11 games, including seven straight. During the losing streak, two home games drew more than 6,500 fans. It was becoming obvious: the Mallards' won-loss record mattered little to their fans.

"There were glimpses of that beginning in 2002. The team wasn't good, but we had good crowds," Stenman said. He added that the Mallards game experience meant more than the game. "That's what you want. That's the beauty of lower level 'minor league' sports. You can't predict wins or losses. If you win, it's a positive, but it doesn't define the team's success."

Stenman said he learned something valuable from a friend, Joe Schwei (the former owner of the Mankato Moon-Dogs), who worked with the WNBA's Minnesota Lynx. Schwei said a team at the highest level of pro sports drew fans with wins, not promotions. "They tried some of the wacky promotions and it didn't matter," Stenman said. "I thought there were more similarities between pro sports and us before that."

So, the Mallards gleefully held the World's Largest First Pitch and had 5,127 fans toss the ball from the mound. That easily beat the 2005 record held by the Class-A Florida State League Brevard County Manatees, which had 950 fewer ceremonial first pitches.

Warner Park, 2006.

And the Mallards kept the Duck Blind going strong and attracted national media publicity. *Sports Illustrated* sent two writers on a Midwest baseball road trip, and in the magazine's online blog, they raved about the Mallards party zone. "The price on our ticket stubs was $32, for a right-field seat on a wooden bleacher, at a college summer league game in which we had no prior knowledge of any of the players. Yet we didn't consider this a rip-off, for one reason: We were in a section called the Duck Blind, and we'd never watched nine innings like this before." The article praised the Duck Blind's atmosphere and gung-ho patrons.

The Mallards also organized an exhibition game, which featured several ex-big leaguers. Twenty years removed from his playing days, slugger Dave Kingman, then 57, hit a line-drive double so hard off the Duck Pond's left-field wall that fans leapt from their seats.

A dramatic turnaround in the season's second half allowed the Mallards to inch their way into the playoffs despite a 36-32 overall record. A crowd of 7,496 on an August Sunday afternoon helped push the Mallards to a crucial 5-3 victory in the playoff race.

The fans' enthusiasm rubbed off on the Mallards players. After his second year in Madison, pitcher Adam Mills told *Baseball America* magazine, "My catcher and I played there two summers in a row, and everybody gets so tired of us talking about it. I promise you, there is no better place to play over the summer than Madison."

Kris Rochelle, Adams' teammate with the University of North Carolina at Charlotte and a future Detroit Tigers draft pick, concurred. "As far as the fan base, this is the best place to play."

The next season, Mills was drafted by the Boston Red Sox

in the eighth round and received a $25,000 signing bonus. He spent four years in the minor leagues and concluded his career in 2010 with the Triple-A Pawtucket Red Sox. After earning All-America honors in 2007, Mills' number was retired by the University of North Carolina at Charlotte in 2010.

AFTER ANOTHER RECORD season by drawing more than 205,000 fans, the Mallards seemed in good negotiating position to dramatically remodel the Duck Pond. By late December 2006, the Mallards had done preliminary negotiations with city officials, with the team offering to pay $2 million of the $4 million cost. Another $800,000 had been set aside by the city for Duck Pond improvements. That left a $1.2 million gap, with Mallards and city officials suggesting that selling the ballpark's naming rights was an option. The Mallards also wanted to control the Duck Pond's scheduling, in part, to book more concerts after the success of the Bob Dylan and Willie Nelson's double bill.

"The old grandstand was steel and wood. It was three different constructed parts of the stadium. They were not very functional. They didn't have a safe, useful life left," Stenman said. "It's an uncomfortable place to play from a sun perspective. Our stadium, to this point, is asymmetrical because a lot of fans don't like third-base side because of the setting sun."

The Mallards never threatened to depart the Duck Pond; Schmitt would not do that. Concerns about groundwater issues and rising cost estimates, however, initially slowed project plans. But the biggest issue was simply bad timing, Stenman said, caused by an impending severe national financial downfall. Still, an alderman, Michael Schumacher, whose district touched Warner Park, pushed for two years to have the Mallards pay considerably more money for Duck Pond renovations—and when he finally supported the project, he added snidely that it would not become "Warner World."

Warner Park includes a recreation center, wooded paths and softball and soccer fields. But the Mallards and the Duck Pond were an undeniable financial, employment and promotional boost to Madison's northside, which features the wealthy village of Maple Bluff tucked along Lake Mendota and includes the governor's mansion; a solid, sizable middle-class area; and public housing varieties.

The factor that ended the Mallards' elaborate renovation plans? The 2008 financial bust.

PRESENTING unusual celebrities became another Mallards strength. And they swam deep in the celeb pool. From 1979 to 1985, veteran actor James Best played the bumbling Sheriff Roscoe P. Coltrane on TV's mindless action drama *Dukes of Hazzard* from 1979 to 1985. Coltrane's most famous line? "I'm gonna cuff ya an' stuff ya!"

Before the 2006 season, Stenman was certain: Mallards fans would not want to meet Best. Stenman booked the appearance to help a friend with the Alexandria Beetles, who received a discounted price by booking Best in a second location. Then, two days after his 80th birthday, Best arrived at the Duck Pond in late July 2006, and "Hazzard" fans swarmed the ballpark. Best was a hit.

In 2007, the Mallards continued the trend to present low-rent stars, including 4-foot-3 TV actor Emmanuel Lewis—with ticket prices set according to each fan's height. In a publicity interview before the Mallards appearance, Lewis admitted it would be his first trip to Wisconsin. "All I know about Wisconsin I learned from (TV's) *Laverne & Shirley*," he said, "and it's cold there in the winter." The Mallards staff did not stop. They also booked Dustin Diamond, the high-voiced character Screech on TV's *Saved by the Bell* (by then a Port Washington, Wisconsin resident) and ex-Chicago Bears star William "The Refrigerator" Perry. The Mallards staff hoped that Perry would recreate the Bears' dance from the 1985 novelty single "Super Bowl Shuffle." Perry signed autographs, but he was far bigger than his playing weight of 340 pounds. Thirteen years after his career ended, Perry arrived at the Duck Pond unable to dance. "He didn't move a whole lot," Stenman said.

For popularity, no one topped Peter Mayhew, the 7-foot-3 actor who played Chewbacca in the "Star Wars" film series. Almost always, the Mallards did not pass fees to the fans for special guest autographs. Mayhew, who understood "Star Wars" fan mayhem well, charged $20 per signature—in addition to his base appearance fee—and he signed about 1,000 autographs over three hours.

The Mallards also featured games with Mikey the Monkey, who ran around the bases, and held the "World Frogleg Eating Championship" when they played the Green Bay Bullfrogs.

During the 2007 season, the Mallards gave away Stenman's former car, a 1989 Pontiac Firebird, that he drove as a teen. The vehicle sat in a remote Minnesota shed where his parents lived. His parents were happy to have it gone. A raffle to win the car was held during the last few weeks of the season.

The Mallards had the car repainted and repaired. They

even remodeled the interior, which had been eaten considerably by mice. The mice, however, left a rancid smell and repeated washings diminished but did not eliminate the problem. The raffle raised $5,000 for East Madison Little League —and, many years later, the car could still be spotted being driven around the city.

"Every year," Schmitt said about the Mallards, "got goofier and better."

The Mallards also featured zany baseball stunts, from launching water balloons into the crowd to blueberry pie eating contests to dizzy bat races, which pitted two (usually buzzed) contestants who would spin multiple times with their forehead on a bat, then stagger awkwardly toward a finish line.

"I never liked that," Schmitt said of the dizzy bat race. "I would hold my breath, 'Just get 'em away from the damn dugout.' I told players, 'If they come near the dugout, push 'em or catch 'em.'"

Baby races were also popular. "Some baby was hungry or coaxed by a parent and took off like a shot," Schmitt said, "and sometimes not. Sometimes, we'd have four babies that looked at each other like, 'What the hell are we doing out here?'"

And, yes, the Mallards played baseball and honored the game. Minnie Miñoso, a 2022 Hall of Fame selection, appeared at an early August 2007 game. Miñoso wore a cap with the inscription: "First hit: 5-4-49." That hit was in the major leagues, which maintained its color line until 1947 and kept players like Miñoso in the Negro Leagues longer than necessary. A nine-time All-Star, Miñoso also had at least one official at bat in big-league games across five decades. The last one, in 1980, was engineered by Stenman favorite, Chicago White Sox owner Bill Veeck.

The Mallards also honored Ryan Spilborghs, who played in the team's first season and entered his third year with the Colorado Rockies. Rather than a bobblehead, the Mallards created a Spilborghs' figurine with him diving for a baseball. It was a sharp tribute, and the Mallards gave the figurine to fans aged 14 and under in 2007. Spilborghs, in turn, kept one in his Rockies' locker.

Near the end of the 2007 season, the Mallards made their biggest promotional splash. The team reached one million fans in early August, and the Mallards marketing machine was ready. On a Thursday night, the team opened its 20-foot-tall green iron entrance at 5:30 p.m. At 6:08 p.m., the millionth fan walked in. It was ten-year-old John Olsen of Elkhorn, located more than an hour from the Duck Pond. He received the honor after he entered with his parents and four siblings. Confetti poured atop the boy as he stepped through the gate.

The Mallards presented Olsen with a specially made (though oversized) black-and-green Mallards jersey, featuring the number "1,000,000" on the front and the back. Of course, Olsen threw out the game's first pitch.

But the most amazing prize for Olsen was unveiled at the start of the 2008 season. The Mallards commissioned a statue of Olsen giving a high five to Maynard, the Mallards mascot, and placed it near the Duck Pond's entrance.

Although it took the Mallards nearly seven years to reach one million fans, it would be midway through the next five seasons to celebrate the two millionth fan, whose prize package included getting to dance onstage with the rock band Flaming Lips during a concert at the Duck Pond.

In 2008, the Mallards expanded its lineup of B- and C-list celebrity appearances at games, booking everyone from Anson Williams, Potsie on *Happy Days*, to Jerry Mathers of TV's vintage *Leave It to Beaver*, to *Ghostbusters* actor Ernie Hudson. They even featured William Hung, an *American Idol* contestant who achieved "fame" briefly on the program's heyday for performing an enthusiastic, but awful, version of Ricky Martin's "She Bangs." Hung appeared at five Northwoods League ballparks, including the Duck Pond, that season.

The Mallards staff explored booking action star Mr. T, but his initial fee request was absurdly high: $100,000. "It was negotiable," Stenman said with a laugh, "but when you start at $100,000 we're not going to get them down anywhere to where we need to get them."

In 2008, the team gave the first 1,000 women at a Saturday night game Mallards scoopers for a jewelry contest. Called Diamond Dig, the promotion was just that: After the game, nearly 1,000 fans dug the infield dirt with the scoopers searching for a real diamond, hidden by the Mallards staff the night before. "It got better and better each year we did it," Schmitt said. Only once did the dig drag on, he added. "Our PA guy (Aaron Sims) finally said, 'It's between first and second.' That moved it along."

Also, the Mallards partnered with Stoddard's Meats to host a pregame promotion by creating a 60-foot, six-inch bratwurst from home plate to the pitcher's mound with connecting custom grills and linking the brat in its casings. When grilled, the brats were cut into small chunks, placed on buns and sold to the fans. The money raised was donated to various local charities.

Baseball was not forgotten. A couple of weeks later, the Mallards welcomed retired umpire Bruce Froemming, a Milwaukee native who is one of three umps to work more than 5,000 major-league games, to the Duck Pond, where he signed autographs with an inscription of his accomplishment.

BUT NO ONE created a bigger splash at the Duck Pond in 2008 than Gary Coleman, the diminutive actor from the hit TV sitcom *Diff'rent Strokes*, which ended its successful run in 1986. Coleman signed an honorary contract to "play" for the Mallards, and ESPN's *SportsCenter* mentioned the story, the first time that the Mallards landed on the network's popular newscast.

Stenman had an elaborate idea for Coleman's appearance at the Duck Pond. He wanted Coleman to enter the batter's box as if he would have an official at-bat. A detailed script was written.

"The idea was we would give him an illegal bat and have the umpire throw him out of the game before he had an actual at-bat. The league would never let us do an official at-bat. The league takes baseball seriously," Stenman said. "I talked to Coleman's agent and told him the idea. The agent said, 'I'm not sure. (Coleman) won't commit to it. But he's doing the appearance. He'll be there.'"

Coleman arrived at the Madison airport on a Friday morning, 12 hours after ESPN mentioned Coleman's baseball "contract" with the Mallards. "He hadn't committed to the at-bat," Stenman said. The agent told Stenman, "He won't give me an answer on doing it. The best you can do is try to talk him into it when you meet him."

The Mallards rented a limousine for Coleman's arrival, and Stenman greeted Coleman at the airport and joined him in the limo's backseat. Stenman had done research on Coleman's interests and learned that he loved model trains, especially Lionel Trains.

"So, I bought a nice Lionel Train locomotive," Stenman said, "and I had our sign company take a picture of Gary Coleman and design this really nice custom Lionel Train with his name and picture on it as a gift."

Coleman and Stenman sat in the limo's backseat and Stenman said, "We're super excited to have you here." Stenman gave him the dazzling train as a present while the limo headed toward Coleman's hotel. He also gave him a Mallards uniform with his name on the back.

"I said, 'Gary, we'd love for you to do this at-bat tonight. It will be so much fun.' We have a script built for it. Our umpires are on board. It will be great."

Coleman said, "Vern, I'm not doing it. This is ridiculous. You're making fun of me." Stenman's script made no reference to Coleman's height. Still, the actor, then 40, was unhappy, but he was set to sign autographs during the appearance.

The Mallards had agreed to pay Coleman's flight expenses and $5,000, which edged toward a higher amount than most of the team's special guests, to do the appearance. The limo neared the hotel, and Stenman felt like he lost the opportunity to have Coleman make an "at-bat."

"Gary," Stenman asked, "what do we have to do to get you to do this?" Coleman declined again.

Then Stenman tried one last appeal: "What if we pay your appearance fee in cash now instead of a check?"

Coleman quickly brightened up. "Okay!"

Stenman went immediately to the bank, got $5,000 in cash and gave it to Coleman. As the game was about to start, Coleman agreed to the stunt's script.

"We put a wireless mic on him, and a wireless mic on the umpire," Stenman said. It was the Northwoods League's actual umpire, and Coleman and the ump agreed to use the script. So, Coleman stepped out as the Mallards' leadoff batter in the bottom of the first inning. He held the bat in the batter's box and even pointed to deep outfield, a nod to Babe Ruth's "called" home run. The crowd gave him a rousing ovation.

Gary Coleman pleads his case.

The opposing coach, Dale Varsho of the Eau Claire Express, was in on the joke. Varsho followed the script and jumped out of the dugout to complain to the ump. "The bat is illegal," Varsho shouted. "There is too much pine tar on it. Would you look at it?"

"What's pine tar?" Coleman asked.

Then the umpire, Jack Herbert, inspected Coleman's bat, tipped it upside down and many superballs fell out of it—as if it was also a corked bat.

"What is this?" the umpire asked.

Then the umpire and Coleman ignored the script. After the umpire tossed Coleman from the game, the umpire began creating impromptu dialogue.

"You're out of here," the ump told Coleman. "It looks like you're going to have a *short* night!"

That line wasn't in the script, and Coleman fumed. It was difficult to understand if Coleman then added to the scene for comic purposes or not.

"Oh, now, you're going to call me short," Coleman barked at the ump. Coleman then kept jumping to meet the ump's eyes—a funny scene for the 4-foot-8 actor. The base umpire eventually stepped in and Coleman left, waving to the crowd.

After Coleman departed the field cheerfully, he sat in the dugout briefly, then went to the Mallards clubhouse, where he expressed anger at the ump's insult. The Mallards later posted the clip—without Coleman's clubhouse reaction—to the then-fledgling YouTube.

"It ended up being one of the Top 30 most popular videos in the world at the time," Stenman said. "YouTube was still new. The clip had 30,000 views; it wasn't millions of views. It was an accomplishment for us." (Through summer 2024, the clip had 141,000 views.)

In the clubhouse, Coleman cooled down and went to a table where he signed autographs. "He was fine," Stenman said. "He was a pro the rest of the night."

Less than two years later—and a few months before his death at age 42—Coleman appeared with his 24-year-old girlfriend and live-in partner, Shannon Price, on a reality TV program. On the show, Coleman complained that Price was not doing anything to make money.

"But I've got to go out," Coleman snapped with disgust, "and sign autographs for the *Madison Mallards!*"

COLEMAN'S APPEARANCE at the 2008 Mallards game drew about 5,000 people, not overwhelming and actually under their season average. Stenman said the Mallards staff learned a lesson about striving for national attention rather than catering to their regional audience.

"We expected a bigger crowd that night," Stenman said. "But we learned a lot from that in a way. Getting national publicity—as much fun as it was to be on ESPN and Fox Sports—taught me it wasn't that important to the Mallards. Being on ESPN didn't really sell us a lot of tickets. We changed a bit after that. Most of the things we've done since then have been focused on Madison and Wisconsin. We cared only about what mattered to our fans. We used experiences like that to help make our decisions about future promotions."

The Mallards, instead, offered the Brat Favre, a nod toward the former Green Bay Packers star Brett Favre, which paired a traditional bratwurst with relish and nacho cheese. And they offered free tickets to the Duck Blind for 250 fans when the Mallards played the Alexandria Beetles—*if* the fan ate a dead beetle. Every beetle that the Mallards offered was eaten. "They came in plastic bags," Schmitt said. "They were edible."

The beetle-eating gimmick was picked up by an international news service, and one fan sent the Mallards a clip from a Dublin, Ireland, newspaper that described the event. "It proved an appropriate gesture," the Irish newspaper noted, "as the mighty Mallards went on to crush the Alexandria Beetles 11-5."

BEFORE THE 2008 SEASON, the staff was rattled by news of the death of 2007 Mallards pitcher Michael Hutts. A junior at Georgia Tech, Hutts died suddenly from a heroin overdose, according to the *Washington Post*, in his Atlanta apartment in April 2008. He was found dead by his roommate, infielder Ryan Tinkoff, who also played for the Mallards in 2007. Hutts' death was jarring, in part, because he was a dean's list student; was five days off his best performance of the Georgia Tech season; and the school drug-tested athletes.

"It is a story of a fine young man who excelled in academics and athletics," Georgia Tech Athletic Director Dan Radakovich said in a statement, "whose life was cut short by a very tragic mistake."

The tragedy was a harsh reminder that players were young, often ranging from 18 to 21. They were talented, but they also faced ample immediate pressure to sign a professional contract before most of their peers finished college. The 2008 Mallards were a typical example. They advanced to the Northwoods League championship series before losing the best-of-three series to Canada's Thunder Bay Border Cats. In game three, Madison held a two-run lead in the eighth inning, but two errors led to three Border Cats' runs and a 6-5 Mallards loss.

CHAPTER 10
"I WOULDN'T TRADE THOSE SUMMERS FOR ANYTHING"

Gabe Courtright signing a ball for a fan, 2024.

BY FALL 2008, WITH PLANS FOR REVERSAL OF THE DUCK Pond ended due to the country's Great Recession, the Mallards still opted to spend $1.4 million for improvements to the city-owned ballpark. The team created new bleachers, restrooms, a shade canopy based on the design of nearby

Warner Park Community Center, and sound systems. Without reversing the ballpark, the Mallards shifted to another idea: Rebuild the grandstand with seating expanded behind home plate and along the first-base line into right field. "We found a more affordable way to address the venue," Stenman said.

Also, the financial crisis in 2008 and 2009 altered the Mallards business plan beyond Duck Pond changes.

"Before 2008, we became a destination for summer outings by businesses. In '08, we started losing that business," Stenman said. "But then we started to see a dramatic increase in walk-up sales. That's how we navigated that time."

In spring 2008, market research showed that nearly 100,000 different people came to a Mallards game each season. The lesson: Many fans made one or two trips annually to the Duck Pond. "When I meet people around town," Stenman said in 2008, "I almost never meet somebody who hasn't been to a game."

In 2009, Mallards attendance dipped below 200,000 for the first time in three years. But that meant a per-game average of 5,992, easily the nation's most popular summer-collegiate amateur team. It was better than about half of the 14 Northwoods League teams' combined averages that season. The Mallards' cleverness still drew fans; the season's new promotions included a between-innings tug of war that moved an 18-foot-tall pair of pants.

AT A POSTSEASON EXHIBITION game in August 2009, Paul Molitor played in the contest between ex-Mallards players and former major leaguers. Molitor, the beloved Brewers superstar, earned a wild response usually reserved for boy bands in their heyday. About 2,000 people waited for his auto-graph, and some acknowledged Molitor's 53rd birthday the next day. Fans' birthday gifts ranged from golf balls with the National Baseball Hall of Fame logo (he entered Cooperstown five years previous) to homemade chocolate-chip cookies. Another couple showed Molitor their albums with 1,200 of his baseball cards.

Nearly 6,500 fans roared when Molitor stepped to the plate for three at-bats, even after Molitor claimed he had only swung against pitching once in the previous five years. Molitor went 1-for-3, with his hit coming off Nick Alsteen, a young Madison man who won the opportunity to pitch to Molitor after he threw the fastest recorded speed—a relatively mild 67 miles per hour—during a radio station's "Speed Pitch Contest" in early August.

A YouTube clip, not produced by the Mallards, showed Alsteen, listed as playing on "Green Bay East High School's freshman team in 1997," against Molitor, who had 3,319 big league hits and was a first-vote Hall of Famer. Alsteen's first two pitches sailed over Molitor's head—and the ballpark speakers blared "Wild Thing"—before Molitor looked at a strike. Then Molitor tore the next pitch into left field for a single. The YouTube clip included Alsteen signing pregame autographs and ended with a ball autographed by Molitor to Alsteen that included the notation "HOF '04."

EAGER TO SEE if they could expand the Mallards' popularity to other teams, Schmitt and Stenman launched the expansion Wisconsin Rapids franchise, in a central part of the state, and joined the Northwoods League in December 2009. They paid the unannounced league fee to put a team at vintage Witter Field, where a Class-A Midwest League team played from 1964 to 1983. Schmitt and Stenman leased Witter Field for $13,000. "It had been on our minds for a long time and was part of our hopes and dreams to eventually be able to do something like this," Stenman told reporters when they bought the team. Wisconsin Rapids would be in the third smallest market of the Northwoods League's now burgeoning 16-team roster.

To handle the Mallards' workload, the team brought back Conor Caloia, the former team intern and their assistant general manager during the team's biggest growth seasons from 2003 to 2006. Caloia left Madison to become director of marketing for the Division 1 Western Athletic Conference, based in Denver, then joined the ex-Mallards manager Darrell Handelsman's Wilmington Sharks, a North Carolina Coastal Plain League summer-collegiate team, as director of operations. While he worked in Wilmington, Caloia chatted with Stenman, who told Caloia that the Northwoods League had an odd number of teams in 2010 and needed a new franchise. Caloia suggested a team in Lisle, Ill., a Chicago suburb, where Benedictine University had a new ballpark. They also mulled a team in Springfield, Ill., the former home to the St. Louis Cardinals' Triple-A club. (Both markets ended up hosting summer-collegiate teams in coming years.)

Stenman then mentioned that Wisconsin Rapids' city officials expressed interest in a Northwoods League team. "Why don't the Mallards do it?" Caloia asked Stenman. "You have the biggest staff in the league." The next day, Stenman started to explore launching the Wisconsin Rapids team.

Caloia, then 28, seemed to be the perfect pick as the Mallards' new general manager while Stenman became the team president and also led the launch of the Wisconsin Rapids franchise, with the first female GM in the Northwoods League, Liz Kern, going to run the Rapids team day-to-day. Caloia knew the Mallards operation, and he returned to Madison with significant experience.

During his second tenure with Mallards, Caloia also earned his master's degree from the University of Wisconsin's School of Business. He became chief operating officer in late 2013 for the company that oversaw the Mallards and their other operations.

Emphasizing how the Mallards remained a priority, the team hired a consultant in December 2009 from a division of Mandalay Entertainment Group, Mandalay Baseball, which owned or operated eight MiLB franchises and had branched out into consulting. The Mandalay consultant urged pushing more advanced ticket sales. Stenman agreed and said many Mallards fans "make their decision at the last minute about us."

The Mallards staff welcomed Mandalay's advice. "We're trying to learn something new every game—learn something new every inning," Schmitt said. "If the fans aren't smiling in the seventh, then it's our fault."

Caloia stayed in frequent contact with Stenman and Schmitt during the 2010 season. Schmitt, in particular, had an unusual communication style. "He sent lists of three- or four-page faxes handwritten with a Sharpie," Caloia said and grabbed a marker to draw an example on a nearby whiteboard. "They weren't listed one, two, three, four...."

A typical Steve Schmitt note, this one sent out to staffers.

Instead, Schmitt's lists were scattershot across the pages with smiley faces. "It was ticket requests or 'a sign's not straight' or 'the food line was too long' or 'In two weeks, I want to put someone on the Wall of Fame.' Then we'd call him at The Shoe Box and work our way through it." Stenman and Caloia, separately, brightened up when fondly describing

Schmitt's uncommon daily faxes with ideas and to-do lists. "When he started texting his lists," Caloia said with a laugh, "it was even tougher to decipher sometimes."

The Northwoods League also took their 16 teams and split them into two divisions by geography, reducing several brutal bus trips. The league added two games to its schedule, so teams played 70 games in 75 days—not including the league's all-star game.

Bobbleheads were offered at seven Mallards games, and they ranged from a glow-in-the-dark player to the mascot Maynard in catching gear to Schmitt wearing a Mallards jersey and holding a baseball bat—not his idea. But the Maynard Evolution bobblehead, featuring three Maynards from generic rubber duck that evolved into their current mascot, captured the most attention. Stenman created the Evolution bobblehead, one of his favorites because it was "a concept that turned a normal night into a great night," he said. "And public radio called us to talk about Charles Darwin to celebrate his 200th birthday."

At another 2010 game, the Mallards presented a traveling display showcasing Negro Leagues history and added to that by featuring three former players, including Dennis Biddle, 74, and 89-year-old Hank "Baby" Presswood.

The other player, Nathan "Sonny" Weston, told the most chilling story from his playing days with the Chicago American Giants. The team's bus, Weston said, stopped at a rural North Carolina gas station, where he walked in and took some food to the counter to pay. A white worker pointed a gun, held underneath a towel, at Weston's face. The worker screamed, called him disparaging names and told him to leave. Weston carefully and fearfully walked back to the bus. On a YouTube clip, Weston told the harrowing story during an interview with Yesterday's Negro League, an organization presenting the traveling exhibit. "Imagine," Weston said in the clip, "I was 21. I wanted to do one thing: Play baseball. I just wanted to play ball."

These players faced relentless racism in their attempt to break the organized baseball color line. And, in the same year that Presswood appeared at the Mallards game, baseball card manufacturer Topps featured Presswood as part of a special set of Negro Leagues stars.

ON JAN. 6, 2011, Schmitt was at former MLB pitcher Ryne Duren's bedside, alongside Duren's son, when Ryne died at age 81 in an Auburndale, Florida, hospice. Schmitt and Duren —a native of Cazenovia, Wisconsin, about 50 miles north of Black Earth—became close friends for more than three decades, after Duren's tumultuous playing days when his 10-year big-league and 7-year minor-league career was plagued by alcoholism.

With poor eyesight while pitching, Duren threw 100 miles per hour, launching wild pitches but intimidating batters. He was a three-time All Star and earned acclaim with the 1958 World Series champ New York Yankees, one of his seven major-league teams. Renowned as a relief pitcher, Duren drank heavily, culminating in an August 1965 suicide attempt on a New York bridge. Playing for the Washington Senators at the time, Duren was helped at the scene by Senators' manager Gil Hodges.

In 1968, a sober Duren began working as an addiction counselor, helping dozens of baseball players handle the sport's pressures and providing support to many people not affiliated with the game.

The charismatic and outgoing Duren made many appearances at Mallards games—and helped Schmitt attract several former players to sign autographs in the team's early years. Duren, who lived in south-central Wisconsin, also frequently helped The Shoe Box become recognized by major athletes and celebrities. That was how Schmitt and The Shoe Box landed countless autographed pictures of everyone from boxing sensation Earnie Shavers to country legend Roy Clark.

Duren also welcomed Schmitt as a guest at several New York events, where stories flowed from Yankees' stars, ranging from Don Larsen, who pitched a perfect game in the World Series, to Hall of Famer Whitey Ford.

"I wouldn't ask someone for an autograph," Schmitt said. "(Ryne) knew everyone, and he was not bashful."

THE MALLARDS CHANGED their logo from daffy duck to stern-faced duck in 2011. They also changed managers. C.J. Thieleke—a former University of Iowa star infielder and a late-round Minnesota Twins draft pick who led the Mallards to two runner-up finishes in 2005 and 2008—concluded a five-year run as manager.

Greg Labbe, who guided the Rochester Honkers to a Northwoods League title, was named manager. Labbe also coached baseball and taught math at a private Christian high school in Jacksonville, Florida.

Equally as important was news that the Mallards sold 85,000 tickets one month before the season started. That tally was significantly more than the 55,000 tickets sold in advance at the same time in 2010.

Renovations to the Duck Pond, though, dominated publicity. In 2011, one Madison reporter described the Mallards home when they took over in 2001 as being "basically a broken ballpark." Major changes to the Duck Pond entering the 2011 season included a new grandstand with better seating: in one area, seats were moved six rows closer to the field; and behind home plate, a few sections were elevated for better views. The ballpark seats were re-purposed from Oriole Park at Camden Yards, the Baltimore Orioles' home. Also, a sharp, walk-in souvenir building was created, utilizing the boards and seating from the old grandstand for framing and siding, creating a building 80 percent built out of recycled stadium parts.

And when concrete was poured atop a brick wall around the ballpark, except the outfield, Stenman and Mallards officials were concerned it was too high. As a result, they had the construction crew cut 11 inches of concrete off it to give fans improved sightlines.

Fans kept coming during 2011, but the Mallards landed out of the playoffs for the third straight year. During the season's first half, they missed the playoffs by .006 win-loss percentage points. But, in the second half from July 8-13, the Mallards lost six games and were outscored 37-6. Early in the season, pitcher Joel Effertz, a former star with Madison Area Technical College, left the team because coaches at his new school, the University of Virginia, wanted to limit his innings that summer. Three other prominent Mallards departed for various personal reasons.

The team's mediocre win-loss record still bothered Caloia, Stenman and Schmitt. "I think a lot of fans see the Mallards and the promotions and all the goofy stuff, and I think they don't realize how into baseball we are," Caloia said in 2011. "We really care about winning and putting on a good show for our fans all-around—not just from an entertainment standpoint but playing good baseball on the field."

For a decade, the team used the slogan "Baseball Like It Oughta Be," which Schmitt favored. The motto, dating back to the 1986 New York Mets, meant more than the on-field play. It extended to the ballpark's atmosphere, striking the right mix of familiar baseball with fresh or unusual experiences, such as celebrating vegetarian burgers to having former TV heartthrob Erik Estrada of *CHiPs* roam the stands.

The crowds, though, kept coming. In 2011, Mallards drew 213,467 fans, nearly 6,300 per game. With the Mallards out of playoff contention, they drew a sellout of 6,750 to end the home season—a loss to the Wisconsin Woodchucks. Still, it was the 26th sellout of the Mallards' 34 home games.

IN FEBRUARY 2012, Schmitt and Stenman took a vacation to Havana, Cuba, after being urged repeatedly to go there by Mallards frequent special guest Bill "Spaceman" Lee, an eccentric and popular 14-year pitcher with the Boston Red Sox and Montreal Expos, who had appeared at Mallards games.

"You guys haven't experienced baseball," Lee told Schmitt, "until you've been to Cuba."

Flights to Cuba from the United States were restricted until 2014, so Schmitt and Stenman flew from Toronto to Havana. They visited Havana's historical sites and watched lots of baseball. In Cuba, crowds whooped it up throughout the games while live music played—and Cubans did the American seventh-inning stretch in the fifth inning. Stenman mulled the latter for the Mallards before keeping the traditional way.

Stenman, though, was influenced by the music heard in Cuban ballparks. The next season, the Mallards presented a Friday night house band, which played between pitches and between innings.

In May 2012, second-year manager Greg Labbe felt immense pressure to have the Mallards win. He described 2011's on-field struggles as painful to him. "Every day, it bothers me. I had a hard time looking people in the face last year," Labbe said. "I felt so bad."

As he scrambled in 2012 to find a starting catcher—several potential players were on teams that advanced in college post-season playoffs, which extended into June—Labbe spoke frankly about expectations as Opening Day approached. "I just think the reason they hired me to manage the team was because I had won the Northwoods League championship in 2006. It's what they want me to come in and do—win a championship."

When the Mallards failed to make the Northwoods League's playoffs for the fourth season in a row in 2012, Labbe was released from the team. Not even a 23-12 record in the second of the league's two halves was enough. As close as his two teams came to playoffs, Labbe said that two second-place finishes "made it more difficult."

Caloia said the suggestion to replace Labbe was made after the 2012 season by Schmitt, Stenman and himself. "Greg did a good job," Caloia said. "But we were so strong on the business side, and we weren't consistent on the baseball side."

Since then, Labbe has not managed for any team higher than his son's 13U travel team, he said, by choice. He joined a Jacksonville, Florida, corporate organization that worked with public utilities companies nationwide and became the company's director of corporate analytics.

"I wouldn't trade those summers for anything," he said in 2024 about his two seasons managing the Mallards. "I had another chance to coach in a different league the following year, but that fell through, and I took that as a sign to move on to other things. I transitioned from teaching and coaching into another career."

In 2012, the Mallards continued to post phenomenal attendance figures, reaching a then-record 217,143 fans. No other summer-collegiate team was even in the same galaxy as the Mallards. They also outdrew 238 of the 261 minor league and independent teams.

Stenman, though, also remembered 2012's lowest point: The worst promotion the Mallards ever did, he said.

The Mallards had success the year before when it featured former WWE stars "Hacksaw" Jim Duggan and "The Million Dollar Man" Ted DiBiase for separate appearances. Former wrestling stars were popular, relatively affordable and available. During an ideas meeting while planning the Mallards' 2012 promotional season schedule, a staff member suggested hiring a touring "little person wrestling" group called Half-Pint Brawlers, which had matches in a ring after the game.

"I wanted to create an environment around the team where

anyone can offer ideas, and it didn't matter if it's an intern or the owner. If it's a good idea, let's do it," Stenman said. "Someone suggested bringing in 'little person' wrestling. I immediately thought, 'We shouldn't do that.' But it stayed on the idea list because I wanted to cultivate ideas. In a few months, the potentially inappropriate stuff like that didn't go through."

Schmitt and Stenman, though, were extremely busy as they continued to oversee the Wisconsin Rapids Rafters and eyed other expansion locations while considering the never-ending changes to the Duck Pond. In other words, the short wrestlers slipped in and landed on the Mallards promotional schedule for July 13, 2012. A pre-game appearance by the wrestlers went fine. Then the wrestlers became rowdy *before* their postgame matches thanks to some adult beverages consumed during the game.

After the game, a wrestling ring was placed in the Duck Pond's tight concourse, and a couple of thousand fans jammed the area. The wrestlers wore wireless microphones and unleashed considerable profanity. "They injured each other. They were bleeding all over the place," Stenman said. "It was a melee. I thought, 'How did we let this happen?'" Stenman and Mallards staff could not reach the stage to stop the event because the crowd was packed so tightly.

"I like to think we built up good will over the years. Madisonians like to complain about things, but we got no complaints," Stenman said. "Some people thought it was a great show. Some people walked around it, ignored it and hoped we didn't do it again. It was terrible and embarrassing."

~

THE 2012 SEASON also saw a fan in a green skintight Morphsuit run on to the outfield from the Duck Blind between innings during a game. Six Mallards employees scrambled to tackle him and kept tumbling on the wet grass in the outfield while the always-animated public address announcer Aaron Sims—distracted and fascinated by the chase—tried to keep reading a list of fan birthday announcements. The wild patron in green eventually escaped, with help from another person in a yellow Morphsuit, through a door in the center-field fence. The comical clip appeared on late-night TV's *Jimmy Kimmel Live!* and generated nearly half a million views on YouTube through 2024.

Caloia said the "chaotic" scene, however, was set up. It fooled Mallards fans and many others. The clip's comments from 2012 on YouTube proved that viewers did not suspect trickery.

The person in the green Morphsuit was an intern for the Mallards who ran track. Available on YouTube, the clip shows a situation that created momentary chaos—with Sims' confusion as public address announcer played to perfection—and fans were fascinated. The YouTube clip provoked media reaction. A reporter for the *Daily Mail* in London called the Mallards office and asked, "What are you going to do with the perpetrator?"

During the "disturbance," Caloia stood behind home plate atop a platform surrounded by fans. "I had to act angry," he said, "I grabbed my walkie talkie and shouted, 'Get security! This is unacceptable!' We didn't want the fans to know."

Sims was the Mallards' lively public address announcer from 2005 to 2013. He also served as radio announcer when the team landed on a commercial station in 2004, and he broadcast the team's road games in 2005 and 2006.

"The Mallards always had a 'why not' attitude when it came to promotions," Sims said. At one point, Sims and the organist moved from the press box into the grandstand. "We were willing to try something just to see what happened. And it worked for most of one season."

Also, marketing director Tyler Isham rejoiced in 2012 when the Mallards offered free Duck Blind admission—if the fan agreed to let tattoo artists place the team's logo on them.

"More than 40 people stood in line. The artists didn't have enough time to even do everyone," Isham said. "But forty people left that night with a permanent Mallards tattoo. It was pretty awesome branding for us. Anywhere they go, they'll tell the story of getting two free Duck Blind tickets for getting the Mallards logo tattoo."

CHAPTER 11
PETE ALONSO
"LITERALLY SCARED ME
TO DEATH"

Pete Alonso at bat.

As a youngster in the 1970s in St. Petersburg, Florida, Donnie Scott practiced at Scotty's Batting Cages, owned by his father, Don. When Don sold the business after Donnie's sophomore year in high school, the family kept one batting cage for Donnie to use regularly.

"He bats for two or three hours a day," said Pete Stroud, Donnie's American Legion team coach, in a 1979 *St. Petersburg Times* article. "That's ridiculous."

But it worked. When Scott, at age 51, became the Mallards' new manager more than nine months before the 2013 season, he proudly acknowledged himself as a baseball lifer. He played everywhere—including stints as back-up catcher on the Texas Rangers, Seattle Mariners and Cincinnati Reds—and managed teams from Billings, Montana, to Dayton, Ohio, to Charleston, West Virginia, to Battle Creek, Michigan.

A compact and broad-shouldered player, Scott loved the game, and he still enjoyed being part of it. The day before the Mallards' 2013 season opener, he explained: "What am I going to do? Go golfing? I don't golf. Fish? I don't fish. I do baseball."

As manager of the Northwoods League's Battle Creek Bombers in 2011, he won a league championship, putting him on the Mallards' radar. When the Mallards staff started their search for a new manager after letting Labbe go following the 2012 season, they initially had one name on their candidate list: Scott.

When Caloia contacted Scott, the Mallards general manager said the veteran coach "pretty much accepted the position on the spot."

Having been a manager in the Northwoods League, Scott knew about the Mallards mania. He also had heard about the team's top-notch reputation. When Scott arrived in Madison, though, he drove to The Shoe Box in Black Earth, where he sat quietly in the store and, anonymously, watched Schmitt's friendly and constant interaction with customers.

"Now I understand things," Scott thought. He wanted to

introduce himself to Schmitt, whom he had talked to on the phone. Instead, Scott stayed back and left with a stunning impression of Schmitt.

"He's doing everything right," Scott said. "I found out why—it's because of his energy and personality."

Donnie Scott having a friendly conversation with the umpire.

Scott also could relate to his young Mallards players and describe experiences from the major leagues to the amateur draft to the rookie and minor leagues. Everything, that is— except college life.

All that batting practice made Scott into a young, super-star slugger. A Little League prodigy, he hit a few 320-foot blasts as a pre-teen with high-level competition. At 15, Scott was chosen as one of the Florida players picked to play a tour-nament in Australia.

Shifting to catcher, Scott starred at St. Petersburg Catholic High School for two years, but he changed schools after his favorite coach, Jim Vigue, was dismissed. Scott's father sold his batting-cages business and moved his family to nearby Tampa, where Donnie could play for powerhouse Tampa Catholic High School during his junior and senior years.

The move worked. A switch hitter, Scott pounded 26 extra-base hits during his senior season. He also socked a two-run triple for Tampa Catholic in the state's championship game and led his team to a 3-0 victory. Almost three months before his 18th birthday, Scott earned considerable notice as a power hitter at a Baltimore Orioles' tryout camp in Florida. Other teams noticed him too. And Scott declared that he was ready to start playing pro baseball instead of going to college.

In 1979, the Texas Rangers made him a second-round selection, the 43rd pick overall. For reference, another high-school star, Don Mattingly of Evansville, Indiana, was taken in the 19th round by the New York Yankees.

Within four years, Scott was a late-season addition to the Texas Rangers roster, so he debuted in the major leagues one month after his 21st birthday in 1983. He played for the Rangers in 1984, then was traded to the Seattle Mariners, where he spent 1985, and hit .220 and .221, respectively. The Mariners released him in 1986, when Scott began his comeback at age 24. It took him six years—after being cut in the minor leagues by the Baltimore Orioles and the Milwaukee Brewers—to land with the Cincinnati Reds.

In 1991, Scott spent most of the season with the Reds' Triple-A affiliate in Nashville. He was brought up to the Reds in September and played 10 games, batting 3-for-19, including an infield single on what would be his last at-bat in the majors.

Still, Scott held valuable memories from the majors. He hit a three-run homer in 1985 off Tom Seaver, and he was one of only nine catchers to throw out all-time stolen-base record holder Rickey Henderson twice in one game. Henderson searched for the little-known Scott the next day during batting practice, and he read Scott's name on the back of his uniform. Then Henderson shouted to him, "Who is this guy who threw me out twice?"

After his playing career ended, Scott received an offer from the Reds to manage the Billings Mustangs of the Pioneer League, the first stop for many minor-league rookies. In his early 30s, Scott coached Billings to three league titles in his first three seasons. Scott was with the Cincinnati organization through 2008 as a roving minor-league instructor and manager. On July 24, 2008, he was part of one of the worst brawls in MiLB history, which eventually led to his departure from the Reds. Coaching the Reds' Class-A Dayton team, Scott argued vehemently with Peoria Chiefs acting manager Carmelo Martinez after multiple hit by pitches and a hard slide in the first inning. A 10-minute brawl between the teams ensued and 15 players and both coaches were suspended. That was not the worst part: At the mayhem's start, Peoria pitcher Julio Castillo hurled a ball toward the Dayton dugout and hit a fan, who suffered a concussion. Castillo was convicted of assault causing serious injury, a felony, and was sentenced to 30 days in jail—a relatively light punishment in lieu of the fact that he faced up to eight years in prison.

"If I could take anything back (in baseball), it would be that day," Scott said in 2014. "I made a mistake and I wish it didn't happen."

A fiery and personable skipper, Scott amazed and startled the Mallards players and staff. In July 2013, Stenman observed, "He's so excited about teaching guys and so authentic. He's very cocky and confident, but very approachable and fun. He's charismatic with the guys, but confrontational. Twice in the last week, I've seen him just scream at players like I've never seen anyone scream at a player—*after* we won games. And, five minutes later, he's joking with them. With the same guys!"

Scott, who began his second decade at the Mallards helm in 2023, explained his baseball focus. "I relate with people who love baseball; I don't really relate well with people who don't. That's why I'm still in this game. I need to be around baseball. I'm here to win baseball games. But I'm also here to develop players. My balance is in development and winning."

THE 2013 MALLARDS roster included several notable players. Tate Matheny, son of St. Louis Cardinals' manager, Mike Matheny, stayed at Schmitt's lakefront home in Stoughton, a Madison suburb, that summer. Tate's roster spot led to a friendship between Mike Matheny and Schmitt, but it also helped the Mallards on the field: Tate helped the Mallards start quickly that season and hit .280. (Tate later spent seven years in the minor leagues, with one of his last big hits a 481-foot home run in Triple-A.)

The Mallards also featured 6-foot-8, 270-pound pitcher Taylore Cherry, a University of North Carolina player who had just appeared in the College World Series. As a Mallard, he was the unfortunate recipient of an accident during one of Scott's rants. After a loss, Scott wildly gestured while yelling at the team…then his hand mistakenly hit a gallon jug of Italian dressing, part of the team's postgame meal, which poured over Cherry. The huge pitcher stood up, nearly one foot and 80 pounds bigger than Scott, and looked bewildered. Scott ended the speech and apologized.

Another oddity was pitcher Brock Stewart, who never played his main position for the Mallards. Instead, Stewart rested his throwing arm and batted .298 in 30 games. However, he became a member of the Los Angeles Dodgers —as a pitcher—from 2016 to 2018. He eventually experienced injuries, including one needing Tommy John surgery in 2021, throughout his minor-league career. But Stewart emerged as a 31-year-old reliever with the Minnesota Twins in 2023 and pitched in two playoff games.

Joining the Mallards' top hitters was outfielder Joe McCarthy, who just finished his freshman season at the University of Virginia. After hitting .303 for the Mallards in 2013, McCarthy continued his career at Virginia. He became a fifth-round pick of the Tampa Bay Rays in 2015 and signed for a $358,900 bonus. (During the COVID-hampered major-league season in 2020, McCarthy started three of the San Francisco Giants' first five games, batting 0-for-10 with five strikeouts before losing his roster spot. He played one more season in Triple-A before spending time in a Japanese league.)

Scott led the Mallards into the playoffs, where they lost their first game, 15-0, to the Lakeshore Chinooks, a team based in the Milwaukee suburb of Mequon. After the game, Scott delivered a furious, profanity-laden rant at his players. The manager wasn't letting his players go down without full effort. "He said a lot of colorful things that got us fired up," said outfielder Alex Bacon. "It worked."

After Scott's "motivational" speech, the Mallards won their next four games, including the first two in a best-of-three championship series against the Duluth Huskies. On Scott's

52nd birthday, the Mallards clobbered the Huskies, 12-3, at Duluth's Wade Stadium. Built in 1941, the stadium had an outfield fence in right-center field measured at 380 feet and 18 feet high. No one had hit a home run over that part of the field all season—until McCarthy, who went 5-for-6 and scored four runs, blasted a three-run drive well over the wall.

Schmitt, Stenman and Caloia sat behind the Mallards bench and savored the team's second championship. Scott knew his team was ready after they blared music throughout the 5-hour-plus bus ride from Madison to Duluth. "They were amped from the word go," Scott said.

DURING 2012 AND 2013, Schmitt and Stenman continued to explore owning teams, bringing Caloia into the mix. Before the 2014 season, they added two more—the expansion Kenosha Kingfish and the established Green Bay Bullfrogs—doubling their team holdings to four. As if to illustrate how well their working relationship operated, Stenman said one of his biggest arguments ever with Schmitt was about the Rafters' logo selection. Caloia also joined Schmitt and Stenman as co-owner of the Kenosha Kingfish, which called their mascot King Elvis. The Mallards officials formed Big Top Sports and Entertainment as the group's portfolio grew beyond the Mallards.

All four teams drew well in 2014. None of the others reached the Mallards level, but only one summer-collegiate team in the nation, the Northwoods League's La Crosse Loggers, came within 3,000 attendees *per game* of Madison's 6,138 average attendance.

In 2014, a 6-foot-3 first baseman from the University of

Florida arrived. Pete Alonso finished the Gators' freshman year with a .264 average and 12 extra base hits, earning all-Southeastern Conference honors. On June 3, he appeared earlier than expected to the Duck Pond because Florida lost both games in its NCAA Regional. Stenman's connections with assistant coaches at Florida and Virginia kept a pipeline of promising post-freshman players, including Alonso, coming to the Mallards.

Pete Alonso.

Jaws dropped immediately at Alonso's power hitting. Early in the Mallards season—and despite Alonso being between his freshman and sophomore college years—Stenman asked Scott, "How many homers do you think he will hit in the major leagues?" Scott answered, "Fifty." He was wrong—barely. Five years later, Alonso set an all-time record for rookies with 53 home runs.

When Alonso was a Mets minor-league star in 2018, the New York media quoted Scott comparing him favorably to then-superstar Joey Votto, who Scott coached as a rising Cincinnati Reds' prospect. "When (Alonso) took a pitch, he would stay there for a second, almost like he was taking a picture of it, like he was going, 'OK, got that one. Next!' That really stuck in my mind. I've only seen one other guy do that, and that was Joey Votto." Scott continued, "I had both these guys at 19 years old. I see Pete Alonso in that same category."

In 2014, when the Mallards held an '80s Night promotion, the team brought in former Madison Muskies player and illegally juiced big-league hitter Jose Canseco. Nearly 6,750 fans filled the Duck Pond for a postgame home-run derby featuring Canseco. Alonso defeated Canseco in the semifinal round, but Mallards officials asked Alonso to step aside for their marquee special guest and to allow Canseco to hit in the finals.

That pitted Canseco against the Mallards' Joe Dudek, who had just finished his freshman year at the University of North Carolina. The left-handed-swinging Dudek, age 19, batted first in the Canseco derby and hit six homers, a stunning display of power for a player who hit no home runs or triples in 120 plate appearances for the Mallards that season.

Canseco wore a New York Yankees jersey, an odd choice given that he played the fewest number of games (37 in 2000) for them than any of his six big-league teams. During the home run derby, Canseco, then 49 years old, displayed awesome power, putting three pitches way out of the ballpark and into the parking lot—each was a towering drive of more than 400 feet. In the end, he fell one homer shy of Dudek, who received a high five from Canseco before being mobbed by his teammates. Canseco also accepted $500 to join several fans afterward to bar hop on Madison's State Street.

The season belonged to Alonso, and the Mallards' Scott watched in awe. Alonso won the Northwoods League's MVP award after batting .354 with 18 home runs. When Alonso came to bat that season, manager and third-base coach Scott stepped back down toward the outfield line. "He literally scared me to death," Scott said. "You know how the umpire will be standing in shallow left field on the grass? I was down there talking to him when Pete was hitting. I've never done that with anybody else."

Alonso returned to Florida for his sophomore year, then played in the Cape Cod League in 2015. He played for the Bourne Braves, which drew 808 fans per game. With the Mallards during the previous summer, Alonso's team attracted more fans in three games during the season than Bourne did for its entire 21-game home schedule.

In June 2016, Alonso was drafted in the second round by the New York Mets, receiving a $909,000 signing bonus. He earned $20.1 million as a Mets player in 2024, and he was a free agent the next season. In October 2024, Alonso hit a three-run homer in the top of the ninth inning to give the Mets a remarkable comeback to win a playoff series from the host Milwaukee Brewers.

～

As successful as '80s Night was to the Mallards, another promotion featuring Whiplash the Dog-Riding Cowboy Monkey was wince-inducing during a doubleheader with the Willmar Stingers. Whiplash rode around the bases on a dog's back.

"The monkey had a cowboy hat on and sat in a little saddle," Stenman said. "The monkey was strapped in, but it didn't do anything. It was cringy. It wouldn't be well received now." It was not at the time, either; criticism led many teams to cancel Whiplash as a game promo.

A participant in Office Space Night.

More successful was Office Space Night, which honored the 1999 cult comedy film about disgruntled office workers. The Mallards presented a postgame recreation of one of the film's scenes: When workers smash office equipment with bats. Veteran character actor and Wisconsin native Richard Riehle, who played Tom Smykowski— the unnecessary liaison between engineers and customers—was the Mallards' special guest. Wearing an office-appropriate button-down shirt and tie, Riehle opened the postgame festivities by battering an out-of-date office printer at home plate.

Then the Mallards, after covering parts of the field with oversized plastic bags for recycling and turf protection, let fans smash other useless office equipment with bats. One YouTube clip featured an oddly aggressive fan in a Mallards jersey repeatedly pounding an old printer with a bat. After he destroyed the printer, the clip ended with him telling viewers, "I was fired last Monday."

With the Kenosha Kingfish, co-owner Stenman considered something more outlandish that season for the Kenosha Comets Night to celebrate the historic women's team. The

Comets played at the Kingfish's historic home, Simmons Field, from 1948 to 1951 in the All-American Girls' Professional Baseball League (AAGPBL) of *A League of Their Own* fame. The Comets, like every team in the AAGPBL, wore skirts throughout their nine-year existence. Stenman wanted the Kingfish to play a Northwoods League game wearing skirts similar to the Comets' uniforms. "I asked the league (officials), 'Would you let us do that?'" Stenman said. "The answer was no. I understand that."

One of the Mallards' most unique players was on the 2015 team. Tony Gonsolin should have been drafted by the major leagues after his junior year at St. Mary's College in Moraga, California, before he joined the Mallards. But 1,215 other players, none Gonsolin, were picked in the 2015 draft. So, Gonsolin became a Mallard—one of the rare college stars bypassed by every pro team before his senior year. For three seasons at St. Mary's College, Gonsolin was a teammate of former Milwaukee Brewer ace Corbin Burnes.

After playing in Alaska and Texas summer leagues, Gonsolin, 21, arrived eagerly at the Duck Pond to hone his talents. Before most games, he was the first player at the ballpark and used the batting cage underneath the grandstand. He also set up batting practice equipment, took his swings and shagged balls in the outfield hit by teammates. "The thing that stands out with him," Scott said, "is his work ethic."

Gonsolin's experience helped him maintain his persistence. And he loved the Duck Pond's atmosphere, where the Mallards drew a record 6,358 fans per game.

Tony Gonsolin at bat. He's gone on to greater things as a member of the Los Angeles Dodgers pitching staff.

"Sometimes this game can get serious, but at the end of the day you have to remind yourself that this is a game and it's fun," Gonsolin said, "especially playing in front of these fans."

What made Gonsolin unusual, and may have delayed his entry into pro baseball, was that he was a two-way player. He nearly won the first Triple Crown in Northwoods League history as a hard-hitting outfielder. Then he also made 12 pitching appearances as a reliever.

During his sophomore year at St. Mary's College, he was a finalist for the John Olerud Award as Division 1's best two-way player. "I just want to be a baseball player," he said while playing with the Mallards. "Whether it's pitching or hitting doesn't really matter."

After playing the most games (71) of any Mallard in 2015, Gonsolin returned to St. Mary's College for his senior year, and he hit .307 and pitched in 18 games, including five starts. In June 2016, he was a ninth-round pick of the Los Angeles Dodgers—who wanted him solely as a pitcher, not an outfielder.

He soared through the Dodgers' minor-league system and debuted in the major leagues in 2019. As part of the 2020 Dodgers' championship team, he pitched in two World Series games. Injuries hampered his 2021 season, but he had an amazing 2022 season, earning an All-Star game spot. He posted a 1.42 ERA during his first 12 starts, ending with a 16-1 record over 24 starts with a 2.14 ERA. That put him in some serious company, drawing comparisons to Dodgers Hall of Famers Sandy Koufax and Don Drysdale.

Still bearded as in his Mallards days, Gonsolin suffered an elbow injury in 2023 and required Tommy John surgery. During early fall 2024, Gonsolin began the first steps of his rehab regiment to return to pitching.

THE NORTHWOODS LEAGUE'S 2015 playoffs felt odd but satisfying for Schmitt, Stenman and Caloia. A new rule put eight of the 18 Northwoods League teams in the playoffs; three of the four teams in the South Division playoffs were owned by the trio's Big Top Sports and Entertainment. When reliever A.J. Bogucki struck out three straight batters in the ninth inning, the Mallards edged Green Bay, 3-2, to advance to the one-game division final in Kenosha.

After years of pushing the Mallards' on-field success, Schmitt, Stenman and Caloia had a significant stake in both teams: The trio owned the team in Kenosha, where they drew nearly 2,900 fans per game to Simmons Field, built in 1920 and restored before the 2014 season. In 2015, Caloia, in particular, worked closely with Kingfish general manager Jake McGhee to put together the team, while Stenman was responsible for the Mallards roster that season.

"It was an awkward situation," Caloia said. "I stood at the back of the third-base grandstand. Vern's near me. We're business partners and friends, but maybe our interests weren't aligned that night." The Kingfish won, 2-1, after a walk-off single in the bottom of the ninth.

Then the Kingfish, in only their second season, proceeded to win the Northwoods League title.

BIG TOP SPORTS and Entertainment continued to extend its reach beyond the Duck Pond when it became the operator of Madison's Breese Stevens Field, the historic but downtrodden downtown stadium. It was the same place that Stenman assumed was the Northwoods League's team home in Madison when he drove into the city in December 2000.

On the heels of the Duck Pond's most successful season, no one had any plans to move the Mallards to Breese Stevens Field. And Breese Stevens, which opened in 1926, was more suited for soccer and high-school football—and up to 10,000-capacity concerts. The neighborhood surrounding Breese Stevens was bustling with apartment and business construction. Big Top Sports and Entertainment was a natural choice —and the only applicant—to run the facility for the city. In 2015, Stenman hinted that Big Top may add a pro soccer team, and that happened four years later.

After constant Duck Pond remodeling and ballpark renovations in Kenosha and Wisconsin Rapids, Big Top Sports
and Entertainment was ready to redevelop the ragged Breese
Stevens Field in 2015. The stadium's history included many
marvels: three NFL games, including a 1929 Chicago Bears'
"home" opener, featuring star Red Grange, when the Bears'
spot at Wrigley Field was occupied; a 1931 six-day rodeo;
auto races in 1938; and, since 2013, home games for the
Madison Radicals of the American Ultimate Disc League.

The Mallards and the Duck Pond weren't forgotten. Mike
Matheny, the successful St. Louis Cardinals manager, came to
the Duck Pond on July 9 after the Cardinals defeated the
Milwaukee Brewers that afternoon and watched the Mallards'
night game. Pitcher Luke Matheny was in the Mallards lineup,
and he was Mike's second son to play for the team. After the
game, Matheny spoke at length to the Mallards describing the
motivation it took to reach the major leagues. "He definitely
had the guys' attention," Schmitt said.

The 2016 Mallards lineup also included Nico Hoerner,
who arrived after his freshman season at Stanford. Hoerner
was 19 years old, batted 257 times with the Mallards and hit
.304. Two years later, Hoerner would be the Chicago Cubs'
first-round pick. By 2019, he became a late-season addition to
the Cubs roster and established himself as the team's starting
second baseman, which continued in 2024. Aside from
Hoerner, the 2016 Mallards relied on Zach Jarrett, a six-foot-
four outfielder, who would reach Triple-A for the Baltimore
Orioles in 2021. His father, Dale Jarrett, was notable to race
car fans. Though retired as a pro driver, Jarrett was one of the
best drivers in NASCAR history, and he came to the Duck
Pond to watch Zach that season.

For 2017, the Mallards loaded up with players done with their freshman seasons, hoping to keep players for as long as possible—and find another Hoerner. To the Mallards fans, though, the 2017 season was a success before the first pitch: The team built a better and bigger Duck Blind.

CHAPTER 12
PRO OPPORTUNITIES IN THE SUMMER-COLLEGIATE RANKS

The renovated Duck Blind in its first season.

DURING WINTER BEFORE THE 2017 SEASON, THE MALLARDS unveiled plans to enhance their all-you-can-drink Duck Blind. The team spent over $1 million—essentially a donation to the city, which owns the Duck Pond, but one that also benefited the Mallards significantly—creating a four-deck building in right field. Using 44 recycled shipping containers, an eco-friendly method called "cargotecture," the Mallards gave Duck Blind patrons a better view of the game and took 400 previous general admission standing spots and added seats for them close to the field.

Opposing right fielders have always taken gruff from Duck Blind fans, but Stenman said the Mallards also needed to find a suitable right fielder. "We put a lot of thought into who plays that position," Stenman said, noting that the Mallards player must engage that drinking crowd by tossing balls to them and encouraging appropriate chanting. After the season, *Ballpark Digest* called the new Duck Blind structure the year's best ballpark improvement.

The Mallards also featured an outlandish entertainment lineup in 2017, ranging from Minnesota Renaissance Festival performers to Mr. Intermission (Willis Harris), a touring act who dressed like a security guard, usher or grounds crew member, then broke into fancy dance routines.

Satisfied with Scott as manager, the Mallards staff did not panic after the team posted a 38-34 overall record. And Scott knew he had a young team, even by summer-collegiate standards. Was he more mellow? A bit.

"I'm not a dictator," he said in 2017. "I want (the players) to know that the door is open if they need anything." Some Mallards, he added, finished freshman seasons with college coaches who did not pay much attention to them. "I don't believe in that. You've got to get a kid comfortable in the clubhouse and on the field. And their confidence is the biggest factor."

For the fifth straight year, the Northwoods League held the Major League Dreams Showcase during the season, which included 100 players (and drew nearly as many scouts) who worked out at midday, then separated into teams for a double-header. The Duck Pond served as the home for this event in early August 2017.

Were Northwoods League players foolish about their chances to make the major leagues? Not necessarily. Eleven days after the Dreams Showcase at the Duck Pond, another former Mallard, infielder Phil Gosselin, joined three other ex-Mallards on big-league teams at the time.

Outfielder Derek Fisher was a rookie on the Houston Astros, which won the World Series that year. Fisher appeared in one of baseball's wildest postseason games in 2017. He was used as a pinch runner on second base with two outs in the bottom of 10th inning of the pivotal game five—then raced home for the winning run on Alex Bregman's single. The final score? 13-12.

Fisher had been the Mallards' sparkplug in 2012, hitting .312 and earning a nod as one of the Northwoods League's top prospects after the season.

Also in late August 2017, former Mallard Brock Stewart pitched for the Los Angeles Dodgers, and catcher John Hicks, a 2009 Mallard, was in the middle of a six-year major-league career, most of it with the Detroit Tigers.

And Gosselin? The former Mallards second baseman in 2008 lasted 10 years in the major leagues for seven teams from 2013 to 2022. He played every position in the major leagues, except catcher. In his last big-league game, he pitched to three batters in one inning and got each player out during a blowout. Gosselin, Hicks and Fisher shared another fact: They all played at the University of Virginia and joined the Mallards because of Stenman's connections with a Cavaliers assistant coach.

THE 2018 MALLARDS sent eight players to the 20-team Northwoods League's All-Star game in Kalamazoo, and they joined Scott, who managed the South Division team, because the Mallards won the division's first half. Among the all-stars was Tyler Plantier, who had already graduated from college but, after redshirting, had another season of eligibility left at the University of Richmond. (The next year, he earned his master's degree while starring at Richmond.)

Plantier's father, Phil, spent eight seasons in the major leagues with five different teams and was the hitting coach for Scranton/Wilkes-Barre RailRiders, the New York Yankees' Triple-A affiliate. Tyler, a 6-foot-3, 205-pound third baseman, was the Mallards' oldest player in 2018 and would turn 23 in the early fall. Troubled by injuries throughout his college career but eager to keep playing, Tyler was smart enough to listen to his father.

"We talk all the time," Tyler said in 2018, "whether it's about hitting, living the baseball life, preparing every day, how to be successful as a baseball player. It's awesome. He's great about it."

Plantier also spent two seasons with the summer-collegiate Elmira Pioneers in a New York State league. Combined with injuries, he had the best perspective on being a Mallard. "Everyone has their own things that they have to get through," Plantier said. "But just to open your eyes and see where we're at and go out there—play in front of 6,000 people—that's a dream come true."

Plantier eventually joined the minor leagues with the Colorado Rockies as an undrafted free agent. He spent one year in the minor leagues and played with three pro independent teams, including the Rocky Mountain Vibes out of Colorado Springs. His playing career ended in 2021 after a brief time with Monclova Acereros of the Mexican League.

THE 2018 MALLARDS continued their emphasis on local promotions with bobblehead nights, featuring former University of Wisconsin football star T.J. Watt; ex-Mallard and Houston Astros player Derek Fisher; and suburban Madison's Matt Hamilton, an Olympic gold medalist in curling. Mallards mascot Maynard appeared in dozens of bobblehead incarnations, ranging from Maynard as a firefighter to a cleverly created Grateful Dead tribute. This time, a Mystical Maynard bobblehead presented the mascot riding a unicorn, complete with pooping rainbows.

It was just as effective a promotion as an earlier one from the early 2000s, as Mallards staff spread 1,000 dollar bills in the outfield grabbed from a Brinks truck driving into the Duck Pond. Twelve prize-winning fans grabbed as much cash as they could.

"It was a sunny day," Schmitt said, "then a strong wind came off (nearby) Lake Mendota and blew the dollars all over. Some ended up all the way outside the stadium."

NOT ALL MALLARDS DEPARTED MADISON. A Stanford graduate and three-season Mallard from 2005-2007, Randy Molina returned to the city after playing one season in the minor leagues and another with a pro independent league team. He was a California native, drafted in the 42nd round by the Seattle Mariners in 2008 and named to the Pac-10's all-conference team during his senior season at Stanford.

After spending one season as C.J. Thieleke's assistant coach with the Mallards in 2010, he stayed in Madison and began to work with youth offenders within the justice system. His efforts earned notice by communities and the media in 2018, and Molina continued to work in 2024 with Dane County, where Madison is the county seat, as violence prevention coordinator helping the community's most troubled areas.

THE 2018 MALLARDS earned the most regular season wins in franchise history, up to that point, with 49. That success did not matter in the blink-and-you-miss Northwoods League playoff system. The Fond du Lac Dock Spiders arrived at the Duck Pond for a one-game, first-round playoff and trounced the Mallards, 17-5. It was season over for the Mallards.

About two weeks later, a foot of rain fell on western Dane County and flooded The Shoe Box's warehouse. More than 75,000 of up to 700,000 pairs of shoes in five warehouses were damaged. Schmitt arrived at his main outlet at 5 a.m.—after taking a few hours to reach the building, which was surrounded by a "small river" created by the flood.

"I had to hang on to houses and trees to get there," Schmitt said. When he made it, boots and Nike shoes floated through the iconic business.

Two days later, Schmitt created a tent sale, offering more than 50 percent off any flood-damaged shoes. When the tent sale opened, Schmitt said, a long line of customers stood just like fans waiting to enter a Mallards game.

⁓

INFIELDER JUSTICE BIGBIE returned to the Mallards for a second season in 2019, serving as a sparkplug for another remarkable season. Unrecruited after high school, he joined Division 1 mid-major Western Carolina University, which allowed him to walk-on as a freshman with no expectation that he would play during his first season. Defying expectations were Bigbie's norm. After two weeks of fall practices at the school in mountainous Cullowhee, North Carolina, he became the Catamounts' top hitter during his first spring there.

In 2019, Bigbie arrived before the Mallards' season opener and helped them finish the first half with a 25-11 record and earned a playoff spot with his .348 batting average. The surprising part of Bigbie's success that season is that his mother, Sarah Fallon, traveled with a family member from Virginia to Madison to deliver bad news to her son. Bigbie's mother told her son that her cancer returned for the third time, but she reassured him that she was fine. Bigbie recalled that moment in 2024: "She was downplaying it," he said. "She didn't want to tell me kind of everything. She wanted me to just play baseball. But I knew."

While his mother received rigorous treatment, something she had experienced twice before against cancer, Bigbie managed to keep hitting well for the Mallards and Western Carolina.

Sarah Fallon eventually became a three-time cancer survivor. Bigbie learned her tenacity and perspective. "You get down on yourself when you're having a rough day, but there are a lot of people who are going through (serious illnesses). It kind of puts it in perspective a little bit. Like, 'Hey, this is just a game.'"

In June 2021, Bigbie finished his senior season at Western Carolina, hitting almost .400. After 18 rounds of the major league draft that month, Bigbie was not picked—and, frustrated by following the draft's updates on his phone and not seeing his name, he walked out of his family's Chesapeake, Virginia, home. Moments later, his father stepped outside to tell him the news: the Detroit Tigers drafted him in the 19th round. Since then, he soared up the Tigers minor-league system and, in 2024, was a promising prospect with the Tigers' Triple-A team in Toledo.

"You want to talk about work ethic and adjustability translating into performance," said Tigers president of baseball operations Scott Harris, "there aren't many better examples than Justice."

In August 2019, the Mallards swept a best-of-three series against the Wisconsin Rapids Rafters, then traveled more than seven hours by bus to Michigan to take on the Traverse City Pit Spitters. It was another one-game semifinal, and the Pit Spitters won 3-2.

Due to the condensed postseason and already lengthy regular season, the Northwoods League continued to use that one-game semifinal and single-game championship through 2024.

The Mallards' 2019 season drew 218,866 fans and averaged more than 6,000 fans per game again. As was often the case, the team's on-field success was secondary. After the season, Mallards general manager Tyler Isham proclaimed:

"We like to think, if we do our jobs well enough, the baseball team can be 0-71 and we'd sell out the 72nd game."

The usual promotional onslaught was on display in 2019. The Mallards, for instance, presented pregame puppy yoga and held an in-game baby gender reveal with the father swinging a bat at the "ball," which burst into blue.

Stenman also handled an early-season controversy when the Mallards cut promotional ties with Chick-fil-A due to the popular chain restaurant's funding of anti-LGBTQ groups. "What happened is the discussion started to shift to a spot where people were associating us with things that we really didn't stand for from an inclusion perspective," Stenman said. "We've worked really hard to create an environment that's comfortable for everyone."

Madison's OutReach LBGTQ Community Center executive director Steve Starkley praised the Mallards. "They've been supportive of our organization," he said, "and I'm glad they're making this decision." The Mallards hang a pride flag, supporting the LBGTQ community, prominently at the Duck Pond.

Two developments happened before the 2019 season. Former Mallard Pete Alonso made the New York Mets' Opening Day roster. He proceeded to win the All-Star Game's Home Run Derby and the Rookie of the Year award. And, in late April, Forward Madison FC, a pro soccer team owned by Big Top Sports and Entertainment, debuted at Breese Stevens Field.

Then, just before 10 p.m. on Oct. 17, a fire at the Duck Pond destroyed the team's souvenir and storage building. The roof collapsed. Arson was suspected by the Madison Fire Department, which put out the fire in a few minutes. Damages were estimated at more than $150,000. No one was charged, but the losses were felt by the staff. That souvenir building had been constructed with recycled stadium items left from prior ballpark renovations—the siding, for instance, was formerly bleacher seating—but now that link to the original Warner Park was gone.

A MONTH after the 2020 season was set to begin, the Mallards cancelled their season due to the COVID-19 pandemic. In classic Mallards style, they still offered entertainment and quickly turned the Duck Pond into a drive-in theater— drawing a couple of hundred cars parked on the field turf for regular showings of family friendly flicks, such as *Aladdin* and *The Sandlot* to, by October, the original *Nightmare On Elm Street*. That was fun, but it hardly brought in the income that 200,000-plus fans produce. Also, the Mallards faced 21 months straight without a home game and dropped their staff from 17 full-timers to seven. They usually employed nearly 400 part-time workers during the season. As a result, Stenman called it "a terribly brutal year."

Dane County, home to the Mallards, restricted public gatherings more sharply than other counties. As a result, in July and August, Mallards players comprised a team named the K-Town Bobbers and played 26 times against the Kenosha Kingfish at Simmons Field. During the unofficial games, Bigbie raised his profile with scouts by hitting .380 for the Bobbers.

In August 2020, Schmitt sent a letter to the editor of Madison's daily newspaper and promised a brighter 2021 at the Duck Pond. "Stay safe," he wrote, "and I sure miss you all."

At a Madison City Council meeting in November 2020, Stenman was able to get the Mallards' rental fee for the Duck Pond from $65,238 to $1. Also, that year, the Mallards refinanced a loan to pay for their 2017 Duck Pond renovations.

GIVEN THEIR BOX-OFFICE SUCCESS, were the Mallards loaded financially? Not quite as much as one may think. The city-owned ballpark has seen limited civic investments. Nearly all of the improvements over the years have been funded by the Mallards and are in turn donated to Madison. All in all, the Mallards have invested over $10 million in the ballpark since the team launched. In addition, the Mallards staff was well paid, and Schmitt considered The Shoe Box as his ample financial resource, not the Mallards.

"Honestly," Stenman said, "not once have Steve and I sat down and looked at the bottom line." Schmitt insisted that the Mallards operated reasonably, but he emphasized the fans so much that there was rarely a time when he said no to improving fan experience.

"It's not about the money," Schmitt said. "Anything I make from the Mallards I put back into the park. I can't remember taking my money and doing something with it. For me, it's about the fans."

What gave the Mallards' top officials—Schmitt, Stenman and Caloia—substantial returns were the sales of their three other Northwoods League teams: two (Kenosha and Green Bay) in 2020 and one (Kenosha) in 2022. Financial deals were not disclosed on any of the three sales, but it was certain that those teams' worth jumped significantly in price over the seven to nine years that Big Top Sports and Entertainment owned them.

AND THERE WAS BASEBALL NEWS: A former Mallards pitcher, Alec Mills, who played on the 2012 team, threw a no-hitter for the Chicago Cubs on Sept. 13, 2020. Mills, a University of Tennessee-Martin player, pitched only two games for the Mallards before being selected in the 22nd round of the MLB Draft and departed in June 2012. With the Mallards, he struck out 17 batters and had a 1.73 ERA in his two starts. It took Mills 679 innings pitched over seven years in the minor leagues before he reached the big leagues. His major-league career included three games with the Kansas City Royals and one with the Cincinnati Reds, which sandwiched five partial years with the Cubs.

A college walk-on who had lasted more than six innings only once before in the major leagues, Mills was happily dumbfounded after the no-hit game. "I didn't really know how to celebrate," he said.

CHAPTER 13
THE WORLD'S LARGEST BRANDY OLD FASHIONED SWEET

Vern Stenman yielding the baseball mixer for the world's largest brandy old fashioned sweet.

WHILE THE MALLARDS WERE AWAY IN 2020, STENMAN AND his staff hired a Madison firm, Planet Propaganda, to create a new logo—the team's third—and helped them to rebrand the club. The result was a busy but wonderful vintage logo:

Maynard looked happy at the plate, which was cleverly made of cheese, and his wing points toward Madison's Northside. The Mallards couldn't fight COVID, but they were ready when the ballpark gates reopened.

At the 2021 season's start, COVID prevention required the Mallards to use only 28 percent of their grandstand to enforce social distancing. When that restriction loosened, fans were leery to return to crowded events. The Mallards managed to attract 3,450 fans per game in the modified season.

And someone stole Maynard's head off from atop the life-sized statue, created in 2008, of the mascot giving a high-five to the team's young one-millionth fan. The statue was unique because Maynard's head was an oversized and heavy "bobble-head," but not metal. That allowed the brazen thief to yank it from massive springs *during* a Mallards game. Workers chased the person, but they were too far away in the team's parking lot. The theft of Maynard's head received a fair amount of publicity, and the Mallards offered $500—in free ballpark hot dogs!—as a reward for help getting it returned. That never happened. The statue has been remodeled and will return to The Duck Pond during the 2025 season.

The team still soared into the playoffs and won a best-of-three first-round series. Then, just as in 2019, they traveled for a one-game semifinal against the Traverse City Pit Spitters in Michigan. The Pit Spitters rolled over the Mallards 6-2.

Scrambling to bounce back from two COVID-plagued seasons, the Mallards amped up efforts to regain fans. It worked as smoothly as the team's many beer taps. In 2022, the Mallards urged countless groups to attend games at the Duck Pond, and everyone from a dog-rescue organization to 700 people associated with the Catholic Diocese of Madison brought fans. (The latter was given a closed tent for brief worship.) Overall, attendance jumped to 5,550 fans per game, but the Mallards suffered their worst record on the field with a 26-46 mark. There was a revolving door at pitcher, and the Mallards used many position players on the mound for one or two games. By season's end, 42 different pitchers for the Mallards recorded at least one inning.

Second baseman JT Mabry was one of the position players needed as a relief pitcher for two games. Mabry, however, became the 2022 team's first minor leaguer. He also played for the Mallards in 2019 before starting his college career at Middle Tennessee State—and returned to the Mallards three years later. In 2024, he played third base for the nearby Class-A Beloit Sky Carp, affiliated with the Miami Marlins. Also on that team: JJ Wetherholt, who went on to earn Big 12 Conference Baseball Player of the Year honors in 2023 and was a 2024 first-round draft choice of the St. Louis Cardinals.

In 2022, Stenman hired a recruiting coordinator, a former Wisconsin Woodchucks' manager, to put together the roster. That gave Stenman more time to help generate large crowds again and to help rebound from COVID-hampered seasons. The experiment lasted only one year as the Mallards were 20 games under .500; and Stenman returned to his vast college network to form the roster in 2023 and beyond.

In August 2022, the Savannah Bananas, a summer-collegiate team, completed their seventh year and last season in the Coastal Plain League. A growing national sensation, the Bananas developed an oddball, dance-heavy version of baseball. The Bananas got bored with the baseball, so they changed the rules. They created a game with more competition than the Harlem Globetrotters, their basketball counter-part, but the Bananas provide the Globetrotters' same showmanship.

As the Bananas, with their well-paid players and on-field baseball circus, packed ballparks across the country in 2023, Stenman focused on making the Mallards experience as enter-taining as possible without putting a pitcher on stilts.

Stenman and Bananas owner and creator Jesse Cole met in the mid-2000s and saw each other through 2010 as part of a group formed to discuss summer-collegiate marketing. Like Stenman, Cole seemed eager to focus teams on fun and enter-tainment.

"You could see the singular focus from him," Stenman said. "He was more passionate about it than others were. A lot of people weren't as serious as now. He had a fire."

Stenman saw two sides to the Bananas' rise. "Some of what they're doing is brilliant. I love fans catching a foul ball for an out. Some is lowest common denominator. Some of my staff went to a game, and they got the feeling it was not 'fan first' but 'social media first.'"

The Bananas' success has been fueled, in significant part, by 8.8 million followers on TikTok. Stenman has not seen a Bananas game in person. "I watched a game on TV with my kids. It was…fine," he said. "It gets people talking about baseball. I like that. If the Bananas create baseball fans, that's great. I don't have any personal interest to go to a (Bananas) game—and I love going to games."

Maverick entertaining Duck Pond fans in 2023.

The 2023 Mallards clicked on all cylinders. The team added Maverick the bat dog, an energetic and entertaining Alaskan Malamute, who promptly picked up the players' wood bats and delivered them, with multiple playful spins, back to the dugout. Maverick's trainer Jayson Fogle said the dog was ready for his debut. "But I didn't know how he would perform with a live game, with crowd, with everything," Fogle said. "I sent him out for the first bat, and I couldn't have asked for a better outcome. He grabbed the bat and came back. By the second time he was out, the crowd was making noise for him, and he absolutely loved it." Maverick became such an immediate sensation that Mallards made the dog their first bobblehead—that spun around like Maverick—in 2024.

The media also enjoyed featuring Maverick, and the Mallards staff still appreciated coverage. Four different Madison TV newscasts profiled Maverick and his trainer. But social media—Facebook, Instagram, TikTok and others—for several years became the Mallards' most effective way to reach and to inform fans about team news. The Mallards' highlights easily lent itself for social media snippets and promotion. In one TikTok clip, a husky male Mallards fan danced between innings in a tutu and twirled a long ribbon as the packed Duck Pond crowd roared. Still, the Mallards' social media was more likely to showcase an actual game highlight rather than off-field stunts.

As a result, ESPN's *SportsCenter* presented a Mallards defensive play in 2023. Shortstop Cal Fisher, fresh out of a small high school in rural Deerfield near Madison, played with the Mallards before his freshman year at Florida State University. As a Mallard, Fisher earned ESPN's number two "Play of the Day" for his stunning no-look swipe tag to stop a stolen base.

Also, a dazzling postgame light show with 150 drones sold out the 6,750-person capacity Duck Pond. And wrestler Kurt Angle—who won a gold medal at the 1996 Olympics, then spent two decades as a popular WWE performer— happily sported a snug Mallards T-shirt during his appearance, signing autographs for a big crowd. Guest celebrities with free time had been limited in recent years, but the former pro wrestlers always drew fans.

And baseball icons were not forgotten. Forty-year Chicago White Sox organist Nancy Faust, age 76 in 2023, performed during a Duck Pond game.

Mallards crowds also swarmed back when the team created the world's largest brandy old fashioned, a longtime favorite drink at Wisconsin restaurants. (Sweet, of course.) The Mallards staff poured 230 1-liter bottles of brandy, 182 bottles of lemon-lime soda and 10.5 gallons of cocktail syrup. Mixed with 500 orange slices and 5 gallons of cherries, the cocktail was stirred with a six-foot baseball mixer resembling a baseball bat in the 325-gallon inflatable glass. Ice cubes were so big they had to be brought in with a wheelbarrow.

As part of the brandy old fashioned promo the Mallards took the field as the Old Fashioneds, compete with custom jersey, caps and sleeve logo.

"I would rather do that promotion," Stenman said, "over doing something like (2008's) Gary Coleman-type promotion again. We want to be Wisconsin as much as possible. The (giant) drink was a silly thing, but hopefully it was memorable."

On YouTube, a longtime baseball fanatic named Ballpark Hunter produced a glowing 12-minute video of the Duck Pond and the Mallards' game day experience. "I gotta tell you, it's one of the ballparks you need to see, not just in the North-woods League, but all of your baseball travels. (The Duck Pond) is truly a fun atmosphere. They took an old, junky ballpark left behind by the minor leagues and a pro independent league and really fixed it up."

A summer-collegiate record of 228,692 fans attended the Mallards' 36 games at the Duck Pond. The per-game average missed the Mallards' previous record of 6,358 in 2015, when they had 34 home games, by just five fans for each contest. Samantha Rubin came on board in late 2021, and by the end of 2022 she was promoted to become the first female GM in Mallards history, overseeing the Mallards' return to solid attendance numbers by 2023.

"Their enthusiasm trickles down on the field to us," Scott said. "The people here are right on top of you, and they can hear you sneeze."

Many former Mallards did not forget their experience with the team. Former Mallard Ryan Rogowski—who played on the team in 2004 and 2005 (earning league MVP honors for the latter season)—brought 200 young players and their parents to a game at the Duck Pond in 2023. The large group from Michigan, where Rogowski is a baseball instructor, had been traveling from a Midwest tournament and stopped to attend a Mallards game. In 2014, Rogowski's jersey number 5 was one of five numbers retired by the team.

After a three-game losing streak in July 2023, the Mallards set a franchise record for runs when they scored 26 times in a battering of the Wisconsin Rapids Rafters. The turnaround did not shock Scott.

"I'm a mentality guy. I really believe in how you feel about yourself when you're out there because probably the most important thing for a baseball player is how they talk to themselves," he said. "As much as you take extra batting practice and things like that, you also have to sharpen the mental side of things. What comes first, confidence or success?"

The Mallards lost in the first round of the playoffs to eventual Northwoods League champion Green Bay Rockers. But the franchise was as robust as ever heading into 2024.

THE NCAA's transfer portal added another hurdle to keeping a roster together, adding skittish college coaches—who at one time loved seeing their young players develop during the summer in the Northwoods League—into jumpy managers worried about losing players to another school.

Just before the 2024 season, Stenman spoke to a mid-major school's coach, who feared that several of his players could attract attention from large college programs if they played for the Mallards.

"They're worried they'll come into our league and do well and, all of a sudden, they will get offers," Stenman said. "People are telling (players), 'Hey, you should enter the transfer portal. You're good enough to be at a bigger school.' So, it hurts us that way."

The Mallards used 69 players in the 2023 season. By comparison, the 2019 Mallards had 41 total players. Because the Northwoods League played more games—72 regular season matches—than any other summer-collegiate league, teams were allowed to carry a 35-player roster, with 30 of them in uniform.

"Most college coaches want position players to play," Stenman said. "It's delicate with pitchers. We almost need a six-pitcher rotation. If a guy throws 85 to 95 pitches, they sit for five days."

Stenman was careful to avoid filling the roster with the best pitchers he could land, especially if they logged lots of innings during their school's season. "We want the guy who's going to become great *next* season at their school," he said.

THE NORTHWOODS LEAGUE expanded to 25 teams in 2024, adding teams in western North Dakota and suburban Detroit (a travel team, the Mud Puppies, rounded out the lineup for scheduling purposes), so the dream for countless players to be pro players was seemingly endless.

How many Mallards made the major leagues? In Mallards history, 25 former players reached the major leagues—including seven from the 2012 team that was 16-19 in the season's first half. The 2012 Mallards manager, Greg Labbe, was surprised when told that in 2024.

"Seven, really?" Labbe said. "It was an extremely talented group. It was interesting to me how much the league changed talent-wise from my stint with Rochester (2005-2007). We had good players in 2005 to 2007, but the number of high-end players across the league in 2011 and 2012 was impressive."

Not every Mallard who reached the major leagues was a star during their time in Madison. One was Matt Pagnozzi of Central Arizona College, who hit .177 in 40 games for the 2002 Mallards. On Sept. 30, 2009, though, Pagnozzi became the second Mallards player to enter the big leagues. His career was mostly lengthy minor-league stints, but he still played for the St. Louis Cardinals, Colorado Rockies, Pittsburgh Pirates, Houston Astros and Milwaukee Brewers in 41 games over six years. His big-league career ended with a respectable .272

batting average in the major leagues with 92 at-bats and one home run.

About 320 Mallards were drafted through 2024 by the major leagues, although the number of rounds diminished from 50 through 2011 to 40 until 2019 and, finally, 20 after 2021. Another 40 Mallards have signed with major-league teams as undrafted free agents.

Still, the 2015 Mallards, for instance, had 22 players drafted, although only two reached the big leagues. Infielder Nico Hoerner (2016 Mallards; Chicago Cubs) and catcher Jose Trevino (2012 Mallards; New York Yankees) continued to play prominent roles in the majors.

The Mallards' highest drafted player until June 2024 was pitcher Nick Howard, the 19th overall pick in 2014, and the Cincinnati Reds paid him a $2-million bonus to sign before his senior year at the University of Virginia. His career stalled in 2023 after peaking in Triple-A. With the Mallards in 2012, Howard never pitched after throwing in 19 games for Virginia as a freshman that spring. Instead, he appeared in 51 Mallards games as an infielder.

On July 1, 2024, ex-Mallard JJ Wetherholt—who played 12 games for the team in 2022 and reached base 28 times in 52 at bats—became the highest drafted former player. The West Virginia star was picked seventh overall by the St. Louis Cardinals. At age 21, Wetherholt received a $6.9 million signing bonus and joined the Cardinals' minor league system.

What are the chances that a Mallards player—even one as heralded as Wetherholt—will make the majors? Slim, but it's extremely difficult to tell. In 2008, the Mallards' public relations department produced a regular press release called The Quack Guide. At midseason that year, the staff named Mallards outfielder Rob Lyerly as "Most Likely to Go Pro."

Lyerly did. A year later, he was a sixth-round pick of the New York Yankees and earned a $125,000 bonus. He spent four seasons in the Yankees' minor-league system before peaking at Double-A. After baseball, Lyerly became a pastor. In fall 2023, he was named as the senior pastor at First Baptist Church in Katy, Texas, a Houston suburb.

On the other hand, few Mallards seemed less set for a major league career than pitcher Cam Booser, a 2011 Mallards pitcher for two games after his freshman season at Oregon State University. In his Mallards debut, he gave up seven earned runs in two innings. He left the team with a 21.00 ERA. He transferred to Central Arizona College in 2013 and signed an undrafted free-agent contract in June 2013 with the Minnesota Twins. That began Booser's near-impossible rise to the Boston Red Sox in 2024.

For five seasons in the Twins' minor-league system, Booser struggled and the team switched him to outfielder. He had suffered a severe elbow injury, a bike accident that broke his back and a 50-game suspension for marijuana and "attitude problems." He quit baseball in 2017.

During nearly four years away from baseball, Booser became a carpenter—who could not forget his missed opportunities as a pitcher, he said. He regained his previous form and a friend posted videos of Booser's workouts on Twitter (now X). A pro independent team, the Chicago Dogs, signed him in 2021, then were stunned when Booser, now healthy, threw 101 miles per hour in his first appearance.

In 2022, he joined the Boston Red Sox minor-league system, and the left-handed reliever made an unbelievable comeback. In mid-April 2024, he was promoted to the majors and appeared in 21 MLB games through mid-June. A few weeks from his 32nd birthday, Booser was the oldest Red Sox rookie since 1947. On June 6, 2024, he earned his first save. He pitched in relief for the Red Sox through mid-August before an elbow injury sidelined him.

"It's been a long journey," Booser said, "but it's been a good one."

THROUGH THE 2024 SEASON, more than 370 Northwoods League alumnus made at least brief appearances in the major leagues. In 2021, five former Northwoods League players, including three-time Cy Young Award winner Max Scherzer (a former La Crosse Logger), were in the All-Star Game. In the 2017 MLB All-Star Game, the starting pitchers, Scherzer and Chris Sale, were Northwoods League alums and both former La Crosse Loggers. In 2024, Sale's rebound season with the Atlanta Braves earned him a National League Cy Young Award.

CHAPTER 14
BUILDING A WINNING COMMUNITY

Donnie Scott coaching from the bench.

IN LATE MAY 2024, DONNIE SCOTT, WHO TURNED 63 BY season's end, agreed to manage the Mallards, marking his 12th year as coach. Nine months a year, Scott lives with his wife Debbie in his hometown of Pinellas Park, a suburb of St. Petersburg and Tampa. They have two adult children and two grandchildren—and pictures of the latter pair were on his coffee mug. Stenman handled the player recruitment, so Scott concentrated on team development. Third-year Mallards exec Samantha Rubin called Scott "the kind of manager that players want to play for."

Many former Scott players, including retired star Joey Votto, have sung his praises. In 2022 at a New York Mets' charity event, Alonso took the microphone and told a convention center crowd about Scott's profane-filled, clubhouse hitting lesson when the 2014 Mallards struggled. It's a hilarious clip that was posted on Twitter (now X) and featured Alonso impersonating Scott, who got so wound up that he compared overthinking while at bat with sex. The New York crowd roared throughout Alonso's almost four-minute-long, raunchy Mallards tale.

A SELLOUT CROWD AWAITED THE MALLARDS' first weekend home game with 1,000 bobbleheads of popular bat dog Maverick given away. Handed out by four Mallards players, the Maverick bobbleheads were gone in 12 minutes, almost an hour before the first pitch.

The game gave many fans their first look at the team's new videoboard, measuring a colossal 90-feet wide and 20-feet tall. It's almost four times the size of the Mallards' previous outfield video screen—and it featured a sharper image. The Mallards paid $450,000 for the screen, and $300,000 for adjustable artificial turf in the infield, which allowed them to add a women's summer-collegiate softball team, the Madison Night Mares. Four teams entered the Northwoods League's first for-profit softball season, a pioneer like the league's baseball operations in 1994.

*Addie Blomberg of the Madison Night Mares, a big addition to
Warner Park offerings in 2024.*

In early July, the Mallards created a hugely popular night,
featuring a tribute to the late Madison native Chris Farley and
his Motivational Speaker character—Matt Foley, a man who
was "livin' in a van down by the river"—featured on *Saturday
Night Live*. The team played the game in uniforms to resemble
the blue-and-white checkered suit jacket and gaudy green tie
that Farley's character wore. Farley's mother, Mary Anne, and
his oldest brother, Tom, appeared at the game, which also
served as a fundraiser for Recovery Foundation, a nonprofit
organization helping with substance-use disorders.

Kyle Chisholm, the Mallards' marketing director, and
Brent Bartels, the team's creative services manager, were
guests on the website *Cllct* (pronounced "collect"), which
covers the sports collectibles industry. The website recognized
the Mallards' rebranding efforts with the Motivational
Speakers promotion.

Bartels said customers bought the team's Matt Foley

jerseys and hats from nearly "if not all 50 states." Ownership of the famous *SNL* skit is not held by the NBC show because Farley co-wrote it with Bob Odenkirk during their time with Chicago's Second City troupe, a few years before Farley performed the character on *SNL* in 1993. As a result, Farley's estate and Odenkirk own the character's rights. The Mallards staff approached the Farley family and received their support. The promotion allowed the Mallards to donate $7,900 to the Recovery Foundation.

Rebranding the Mallards happened seven times in 2023 and 2024. With players in uniquely designed uniforms, it boosts merchandise sales and provides a fresh, if outrageous, look to the team. In 2024, they played as the Wisconsin Wurst, a nod to the state's popular bratwurst, and returned as the Muskallards, a mythical creature from a nearby lake that's a cross between a muskie and a mallard.

"The biggest thing is, if you have an idea, there's really no way to test how much people will buy it," Chisholm told *Cllct.com*. "It's just one of those things that we have a national angle and we have the Madison angle, let's cross our fingers and hope that people latch on to this."

Even the Mallards' regular uniforms have a clever surprise. Since 2021, the uniforms seemingly have thin, solid black stripes. Look closely, really closely, and each line features a city, town or village in Dane County or a Madison neighborhood. It's a brilliant touch, one that the Mallards adapted from a 2017 suit that ultimate fighter Conor McGregor wore to a pre-fight event. McGregor's suit stripes repeated the same colorful language over and over to his opponent; Mallards designers used the style with more creativity.

Every Mallards item was available in the team's spacious

scheduled 28 road games before hoping that weather would cooperate for their season's first home game. (It did.) North Dakota State finished with a 20-30 overall record in the Division 1 Summit League.

Davis Hamilton (L) and Jake Schaffner (R) celebrate the end of an inning against the Fond du Lac Dock Spiders.

Stenman wasn't surprised Schaffner and Hamilton emerged from a remote college atmosphere. He knew that North Dakota State spent mid-February to mid-March playing games in California, Oregon and Louisiana. As a result, they played many prominent opponents, including multiple games at nationally ranked schools, including LSU and Oregon State. For the Mallards, Schaffner hit a team-leading .351, and Hamilton made the end-of-the-season all-Northwoods League team.

"There's a big hunger from players like that," Stenman said. "We've had large school guys, and they don't understand the culture."

That culture features the largest crowds of any summer-collegiate team as well as the Mallards' many outrageous promotions and customer service, which includes players signing autographs after home games—a long-standing tradition at the Duck Pond.

~

IN LATE JULY, a little more than two weeks before the Northwoods League's snappy five-day playoffs, Stenman met with each Mallards player and asked whether they were going to stay with the team as late as August 15 if they advanced to the championship game. Most players were in; four declined and were sent home.

"Even a year ago, we wouldn't have done that," Stenman said. "Last year, we let two of our best players stick around even though they were leaving early."

A starting outfielder said he would stay, then departed 10 days before the season ended. Shortly after his decision, he announced on social media that he joined the University of New Orleans through the transfer portal. Stenman brought in replacements and still felt good about the Mallards' title chances, hoping for their third crown and first since 2014.

~

SCHMITT SAW EVERY MALLARDS' home game in 2024. He has attended 820 of the Mallards' 825 games at the Duck Pond since they debuted in 2001. What happened during the five absences? A friend gave him tickets to the 2002 MLB All-Star Game in Milwaukee; he attended two weddings, both with the same groom; he saw one of his granddaughter's state tournament soccer games; and a grandchild had graduation.

At the Duck Pond, he sat in a section underneath the press box and off to the side. "It's a comfort zone for me. I'm like a 12-year-old kid when I'm out there. I love it," he said. Schmitt watched games with his partner Jeannie Lemke or friends. It took nearly a decade before he slowed down to keep an eye on games. But, even in 2024, he found himself obsessing on the fans' experiences.

Schmitt felt proud that the Mallards drew another 217,000 fans and more than 6,202 per game despite 13 rain-delayed contests at the Duck Pond. The attendance meant the Mallards averaged more fans at each game than 106 of the 120 MiLB teams affiliated with major league clubs. The team also maintained a better attendance average than 19 of the 30 Triple-A teams, including ones in Charlotte and Hartford, and landed less than 80 fans per game below three other Triple-A teams in Las Vegas, Buffalo and Norfolk.

THE MALLARDS WON THEIR BEST-OF-THREE, first-round playoff series against the Wausau Woodchucks. That meant the Mallards would play host to the Kalamazoo Growlers, who earned a late-season spot in the playoffs, in a one-game semifinal. Pitching woes became glaring in the Northwoods League playoffs each season. There were rarely any off days, and the best-of-three series at the playoffs' start usually drained teams of their aces.

Not Kalamazoo. The Growlers gave up 18 runs in their lone playoff loss to the Rockford Rivets, then won Game 3 to advance to play Madison in the one-game, winner-moves-on semifinals. And the Growlers had Northwoods League Pitcher of the Year, Ryan Kraft, a lefty from Indiana University, waiting for the Mallards. Kalamazoo needed Kraft to pitch in one of its final regular-season games or they would not have made the playoffs. So, the league's ace was ready.

At the Duck Pond, Kraft allowed one hit in seven innings to lead the Growlers to a nail-biting 3-2 victory. (The next night, Kalamazoo won the league title, 8-7, in 14 innings against the La Crosse Loggers in a rain-delayed game that lasted seven hours and ended after 1 a.m.)

When the Mallards' playoffs ended, Schmitt was the last person in the stands. It was an empty ballpark, aside from Scott and Stenman talking to Mallards players about next season in the team's clubhouse. "I'm a big fan, too. It stings," Schmitt said. "The next day is better. Think positive and get ready for next year."

Immediately after the semifinal loss, Stenman planted himself at the Duck Pond's only exit. He started doing this near the season's end several years ago. He thanked fans for coming, appreciated their support and shook their hands. Many fans responded with glowing words about the Mallards season—even after the semi-final loss.

"It's one of my favorite things to do each season because there is a lot of joy from fans," Stenman said, "win or lose."

CHAPTER 15
A LASTING LEGACY

*Vern Stenman, Steve Schmitt and Conor Caloia. Photo copyright
Sharon Vanorny, courtesy Madison Magazine.*

WHAT DO THE MALLARDS DO AFTER AN ENCORE TO AN
encore to an encore? What now—at 25?

They have grown up as an organization. For instance, the
Busch Light Duck Blind, with its unlimited beer as part of the

ticket price, remains as popular as ever. But the Mallards have dramatically improved that right-field area's sightlines, seating and service over the years. It's still raucous, at times, but this isn't the Duck Blind, circa 2004—and that is how the Mallards aged so well. Other improvements keep coming, especially 2024's enormous 20' x 90' videoboard that would be the envy of any baseball team not in the major leagues. More importantly, Schmitt and Stenman's obsession with customer service stayed at the team's heart. Treat fans well for 24 years, though, and their expectations rise. Well, fine, they said. The team's staff piled on promotions, pride and professionalism. It was also doing the little things: Call the Mallards office and an in-person staff member answered politely by the second ring.

On September 17 and 18, 2024, the team's staff closed their offices and turned it into what they dubbed "Duck U." They do it annually to discuss the next season's ideas and goals and to recap the previous season. They tossed up a few 2025 special guest possibilities: a cast member from TV's *Modern Family*; Milwaukee Bucks' player Thanasis Antetokounmpo, Giannis' popular older brother; and Shooter McGavin from the 1996 Adam Sandler film *Happy Gilmore*. For 2025, they also discussed installation of a miniature zipline for a concession-toting rubber duck in right field that would land at a concession stand, allowing fans to receive the souvenir collectible duck with their food and drink. "Every minute or two," Stenman marveled, "you'd see this hot dog or can of beer zipping overhead."

Modest to a fault, they wanted to keep the team's 25th anniversary relatively sedate, fearing that may seem like they were "patting themselves on the back," Stenman said. One fun nod to the past will be a "Frankenstein" uniform, featuring elements of eight different uniforms worn over the years, along with each of the team's logos.

LESS THAN THREE weeks after the Mallards' post-season staff meetings, Pete Alonso hit a dramatic three-run homer in the ninth inning, leading the New York Mets to a remarkable playoff comeback victory and to advance them over the favored Milwaukee Brewers. Meeting reporters after the emotional and stunning hit in Milwaukee, Alonso was asked by a Madison writer about his year with the Madison Mallards. During one of Alonso's finest moments, he didn't hesitate to reminisce and noted how he developed as a player one decade before with the Mallards. "I had a tough freshman year, and for me, I think I found my true identity as a ballplayer in Madison," he said thoughtfully. "That 2014 summer was really formative. It taught me what the minor leagues were going to be like because there's a ton of hours. I had a great manager in Donnie Scott. I had great teammates. I had a great host family." He entered the 2025 season as a returning member of the New York Mets.

Scott, still fiery at age 63, has spent his entire adulthood as a player or a coach, and he clearly savored his time working with young players. Alonso's shoutout at such a dramatic time showed how the Mallards resounded with players. In fall 2024, Scott agreed to return to the Mallards for the 2025 season, his 13th in Madison. "I don't have a bad day when I am up here," Scott told a Tampa weekly newspaper. "I feel very fortunate to do this. For me, getting underneath the lights and seeing the players' success—that is exciting to me. I love the organization. I love who I work for. (Owner) Steve

Schmitt is the reason I am still here. Being a manager in the minor leagues is more complicated these days. Here, they let me do what I need to do. They trust me."

In 2024, the Mallards managed to find a new potential income stream and to establish themselves in women's athletics. Warner Park's new synthetic turf infield with a movable pitcher's mound allowed them to form a women's summer-collegiate softball team, the Madison Night Mares. Four teams entered the Northwoods League's first for-profit softball season. The women's summer-collegiate softball team—with an adorable small live horse named Midnight as its mascot—drew a league-high 1,250 per game, an average higher than 14 of the 24 baseball teams in the NWL, in their first season at Warner Park. Northwoods League Softball also debuted as the first for-profit organization of its kind.

"We sold a lot of merchandise. We broke new ground. Nobody has done a college softball summer league like the Northwoods," Stenman said. "Fast forward 10 years from now and that model will be replicated all over the place." A fifth team was added to the softball league entering 2025.

With the Night Mares' arrival, the Mallards' purchase of the all-turf infield led the organization to develop youth baseball and softball tournaments on open days. The Night Mares' sliding outfield fence also makes the ballpark suited for all ages. Already home to two high school teams, the field will feature 48 teams participating in six youth baseball and softball tournaments. During 2025, the field will have more than 200 games played on it, up from 55 games played at the Duck Pond in 2023.

DUCK POND
ATTENDANCE

(Year, games, total attendance, average per game)
    2001: 30 – 31,166 – 1,039
    2002: 32 – 63,131* – 1,933*
    2003: 31 – 136,751* – 4,411*
    2004: 31 – 154,258* – 4,976*
    2005: 34 – 195,105* – 5,738*
    2006: 34 – 205,896* – 6,056*
    2007: 34 – 205,606* – 6,047*
    2008: 34 – 207,949* – 6,116*
    2009: 33 – 197,723* – 5,992*
    2010: 33 – 194,179* – 5,884*
    2011: 34 – 213,497* – 6,278*
    2012: 35 – 217,143* – 6,204*
    2013: 35 – 217,833* – 6,109*
    2014: 35 – 214,849* – 6,138*
    2015: 35 – 216,159* – 6,358*
    2016: 34 – 205,324* – 6,039*
    2017: 34 – 214,485* – 6,308*
    2018: 35 – 217,070 * – 6,202*

2019: 36 – 218,866* – 6,080*
2020: No season due to Covid
2021: 36 – 124,207* – 3,450 (capacity limited; Covid)
2022: 36 – 199,785* – 5,550*
2023: 36 – 228,692* – 6,353*
2024: 35 – 217,070* – 6,202*
*Led the nation's summer-collegiate league teams

BIBLIOGRAPHY

In-person interviews with Steve Schmitt, Vern Stenman and Conor Caloia during 2023 and 2024 are used frequently throughout the book. Anje Van Roo, Dennis Degenhardt, Greg Labbe, Rich Reynolds, Aaron Sims and dozens of others were also contributors.

Various websites were used extensively for reference and videos in many chapters. They include *Baseball-Research.com*, *TheBaseballCube.com*, *MiLB.com*, *MLB.com*, *NorthwoodsLeague.com*, *MallardsBaseball.com*, *Newspapers.com*, *BallparkDigest.com*, *StatsCrew.com*, Society of American Baseball Research (SABR), Historic Madison, Wi. Photo Group (Facebook), *YouTube.com*, *Reddit.com*, X (formerly Twitter), *Retrosheet.org* and *Baseball-Almanac.com*.

Thanks to Tom Coleman, who provided vintage Madison Mallards pocket schedules from 2001 to 2010; Jim's Kard Korner in Madison; "Madison Mallards 2001-2007," the team's promotional booklet; and Touch of Pride Sales, Monona, Wisconsin, which featured considerable Mallards memorabilia.

Chapter 1

"Summer Collegiate Leagues," *TheBaseballObserver.com*, September 2024.

Seligman, Noah, "Handelsman lights up Warner Park," *The Capital Times*, June 10, 2004.

"Mallards draw 10,061 for win," *Wisconsin State Journal*, no byline, June 13, 2004.

Mosiman, Dean, "City sets limit of 5,000 at Mallards games," *Wisconsin State Journal*, July 6, 2004.

Mulhern, Tom, "Mallards manage to win," *Wisconsin State Journal*, June 10, 2004.

"Mallards top Woodchucks," *The Capital Times*, no byline, June 5, 2001.

"Rain suspends Mallards' opener," *The Capital Times*, no byline, June 2, 2001.

Buragas, Amelia, "Duck Pond threshold," *The Capital Times*, July 6, 2004.

"Summer College League List," *Collegiate Baseball Newspaper*, December 2023.

"Looking Back: Madison Mallards Draw 10,061 Fans for Single Game," *NorthwoodsLeague.com*, no byline, March 19, 2018.

"Ex-Lancer Zink propels Mallards," *The Capital Times*, no byline, June 12, 2004.

Ingersoll, Brenda, "Gates mean Mallards can increase their gate," *Wisconsin State Journal*, Aug. 7, 2004.

Interview with Dennis Degenhardt, 2023.

Interview Anje Van Roo, 2023.

Chapter 2

"League is baseball dream come true for Radatz Jr.," *Post Bulletin*, no byline, June 6, 2002.

Malzhan, Kyle, titled "Dick Radatz Jr. Feature Story," *YouTube.com*, 2019.

Platt, Adam, "How the Northwoods League quietly became the dominant baseball league in the Upper Midwest," *Twin Cities Business*, June 18, 2018.

Semrau, Dennis, "Black Wolf finished, but others interested," *The Capital Times*, Oct. 10, 2000.

Antonen, Mel, "Summer College Leagues Use Different Schools of Thought," *USA Today*, June 24, 2004.

Grossfeld, Stan, "League of his own," *Boston Globe*, July 9, 2013.

Christensen, Joe, "Out of the backwoods: Northwoods League no longer a sleepy summer outpost," *Star Tribune*, Aug. 2, 2018.

Henn, Donny, "Fans turn out in record numbers," *Post Bulletin*, June 1, 2004.

Moe, Doug, "Big leaguer's son finds own niche in game," *Wisconsin State Journal*, July 21, 2013.

Reichard, Kevin, "In 20th season, Northwoods League better than ever," *Ballpark Digest*, July 23, 2013.

"Did Radatz take fall?", *Miami Herald*, no byline, Dec. 11, 1989.

Negri, Gloria, "No Ballplaying Inside House—But Dick Radatz Jr. May Balk," *Boston Globe*, May 24, 1965.

Reusse, Patrick, "Newcomer St. Cloud to open play in college league," *Star Tribune*, June 9, 1997.

"League's VP has baseball in his blood," *Post Bulletin*, no byline, June 8, 1994.

Uhlman, Harold, "Northwoods League no longer just another league," *Think Blue LA*, April 20, 2016.

Civin, Todd, "Red Sox Dick Radatz: Having a Catch With 'The Monster's' Biggest Fan," *BleacherReport.com*, July 10, 2010.

"What is the Cape Cod Baseball League?", *CapeCodLeague.com*, no byline, May 2, 2024.

Grossfeld, Stan, "Dick Radatz Jr. building summer baseball empire," *Boston Globe*, July 8, 2013.

Campbell, Dave, "Northern exposure: College summer league continues to grow," Associated Press, July 11, 2016.

Allenspach, Kevin, "Task force wants to land Northwoods baseball team," *St. Cloud Times*, Aug. 15, 1996.

Allenspach, Kevin, "Northwoods League set for respect," *St. Cloud Times*, June 8, 1997.

Chapter 3

Interviews with Steve Schmitt, 2023 and 2024.

Mulhern, Tom, "Mallards Man," *Wisconsin State Journal*, May 27, 2006.

Hall, Andy and Mulhern, Tom, "Badgers' shoe discounts may violate NCAA rules: After being told by State Journal, university launches investigation," *Wisconsin State Journal*, July 9, 2000.

Chapter 4

Anderson, Eric, "City to listen to baseball offers," *Wisconsin State Journal*, Oct. 10, 2000.

Rogers, Lesley, "Baseball will return to Madison next year," *Wisconsin State Journal*, Dec. 19, 2000.

Mosiman, Dean, "Other council action," *Wisconsin State Journal*, Jan. 3, 2001.

Hall, Andy and Mulhern, Tom, "Badgers' shoe discounts may violate NCAA rules: After being told by State Journal, university launches investigation," *Wisconsin State Journal*, July 9, 2000.

Hart, Joe, "Other shoe dropping on Bucky," *The Capital Times*, Sept. 2, 2000.

Oates, Tom, "Reality slaps Discount Shoes U.," *Wisconsin State Journal*, Sept. 1, 2000.

Mulhern, Tom, "Playing without five starters, Badgers prevail," *Wisconsin State Journal*, Sept. 1, 2000.

Hall, Andy and Mulhern, Tom, "Dayne was among frequent shoppers at Shoe Box," *Wisconsin State Journal*, July 9, 2000.

Semrau, Dennis, "Black Wolf eyes franchise demise," *The Capital Times*, Sept. 2, 2000.

Feuerherd, Vic, "Black Wolf all but gone," *Wisconsin State Journal*, Sept. 1, 2000.

LeBarton, Chris, "Home improvements at Warner Park," *Wisconsin State Journal*, June 1, 2003.

"Madison Muskies," *FunWhileItLasted.com*, July 2, 2021.

Johnson, Lloyd and Wolff, Miles, *The Encyclopedia of Minor League Baseball*, first edition, Baseball America, 1993.

Baseball America's 1994 Almanac," *Baseball America*, 1994.

Mell, Doug, "Muskies might get council OK at last," *Wisconsin State Journal*, April 13, 1982.

"First 6 games at Breese Stevens," no byline, *Wisconsin State Journal*, April 13, 1982.

Falduto, Brad, "The old and new: Breese Stevens, Muskies," *The Capital Times*, April 26, 1982.

Schmitt, Steven D. (no relation to the Mallards owner Steve Schmitt), *A History of Badger Baseball: The Rise and Fall of America's Pastime at the University of Wisconsin*, University of Wisconsin Press, April 2017.

D'Amato, Gary, "26 years later, UW still without varsity baseball," *Milwaukee Journal Sentinel*, Aug. 19, 2017.

"Fishing Fish—Madison Baseball History and the Madison Muskies," no byline, *NorthwoodsLeague.com*, June 6, 2006.

"Madison Senators Franchise History (1907-1914)," no byline, *Stats-Crew.com*, undated.

Cornelius, Lew, "Industrial Leaguers Drop 14-5 Game to Monarchs," *The Capital Times*, July 18, 1947.

"Eddie Lenehan Signed to Manage Madison Club," *Wisconsin State Journal*, no byline, April 9, 1924.

"Alter Playoff Plan or Blues Quit: Lehman," *The Capital Times*, no byline, Sept. 27, 1937.

"Madison Forfeits State Title," *Wisconsin State Journal*, no byline, Sept. 27, 1937.

"(Night) Baseball Opening," full-page ad, *Wisconsin State Journal*, May 23, 1943.

Lucas, Mike, "Breese Stevens a site of historic moments and modern revival," *The Capital Times*, July 31, 2023.

"Happy Birthday, Wimpy Quinn!", *MightyCaseyBaseball.com*, no byline, May 23, 2016.

McCormick, Henry J., "Owens Steps 100 Yards in :09.8; Blues Win Again," *Wisconsin State Journal*, Aug. 5, 1938.

Chapter 5

"United Hockey League attendance," *HockeyDB.com*, no byline, July 2000.

Polzin, Jim, "Younger Doering returns with bat, glove," *The Capital Times*, June 1, 2001.

"Mallards migrate to city," *The Capital Times*, no byline, March 20, 2001.

McMahon, Jason, "Love of the game drives GM," *The Capital Times*, Aug. 13, 2005.

Mulhern, Tom, "Mallards Man," *Wisconsin State Journal*, May 27, 2006.

Reichard, Kevin, "Home of the Mallards," *Ballpark Digest*, June 2006.

Chapter 6

Multer, Mark, "Madison team faces uphill climb to succeed," *Wausau Daily Herald*, May 27, 2001.

"Chucks shut out Madison Mallards," *Wausau Daily Herald*, no byline, June 3, 2001.

"Mallards suspended in ninth," *Wisconsin State Journal*, no byline, June 12, 2001.

"Storms suspend Mallards," *The Capital Times*, no byline, June 12, 2001.

"Mallards rally late, salvage split," *The Capital Times*, no byline, June 13, 2001.

"Hitting, fielding foil Mallards," *Wisconsin State Journal*, no byline, June 19, 2001.

Mulhern, Tom, "NCAA prober was in town, met Schmitt," *Wisconsin State Journal*, June 30, 2001.

Lucas, Mike, "It's all about game, dreams for Mallards," *The Capital Times*, June 21, 2001.

Anderson, Eric, "Around the horn," *Wisconsin State Journal*, June 23, 2001.

Anderson, Eric, "Mallards eager for next at-bat," *Wisconsin State Journal*, Aug. 10, 2001.

"Mallards win big in final home game," *The Capital Times*, no byline, Aug. 4, 2001.

Chapter 7

"Mallards moves," *Wausau Daily Herald*, no byline, Aug. 14, 2001.

Anderson, Eric, "Mallards back for seconds," *Wisconsin State Journal*, June 2, 2002.

Begun, Jake, "Madison ranked 15th drunkest city in nation," *The Badger Herald*, Feb. 8, 2010.

"7 Of The 10 Drunkest Cities In America Are All In One State," *Vinepair.com*, July 2023.

Semrau, Dennis, "Mallards' fun atmosphere taking flight," *The Capital Times*, June 11, 2002.

"Mallards Begin Second Half on Sour Note, Lose 5-2 to Woodchucks," *NorthwoodsLeague.com*, July 11, 2002.

"Mallards promotions," *Wisconsin State Journal*, no byline, May 23, 2002.

LeBaron, Christian, "Mallards fall in home opener," *Wisconsin State Journal*, June 9, 2002.

"Sports briefs," *Wisconsin State Journal*, no byline, July 26, 2002.

LeBaron, Christian, "Mallards fans flock for fun," *Wisconsin State Journal*, Aug. 11, 2002.

Anderson, Eric, "Most signs suggest Madison's college development team is here to stay," *Wisconsin State Journal*, June 2, 2002.

"Mallards, WSUM announce radio deal," *Wisconsin State Journal*, no byline, April 28, 2002.

Zaleski, Rob, "Steve Schmitt: on golden pond," *The Capital Times*, July 28, 2003.

McKissack, Fred, "Ten try out for a job in fowl territory," *Wisconsin State Journal*, May 28, 2003.

LeBarton, Chris, "Home improvements at Warner Park," *Wisconsin State Journal*, June 1, 2003.

Mellenthin, Ryan, "Brewers mainstay nearly became Madison's manager," *The Capital Times*, Aug. 13, 2008.

"All-Star Record!", *NorthwoodsLeague.com*, no byline, July 17, 2003.

Mertz, Adam, "Northwoods stars set to light up the night," *The Capital Times*, July 16, 2003.

LeBaron, Chris, "The show on the road," *Wisconsin State Journal*, June 22, 2003.

McMahon, Jason, "Amid fresh faces, Hall returns to Mallards' fold," *The Capital Times*, June 10, 2003.

LeBaron, Chris, "Ducks on the pond," *Wisconsin State Journal*, June 11, 2003.

"Sports briefs," *Wisconsin State Journal*, no byline, June 8, 2003.

"Record crowd sees Mallards fall," *The Capital Times*, no byline, July 19, 2003.

McMahon, Jason, "Packing the Pond," *The Capital Times*, Aug. 11, 2003.

Mulhern, Tom, "Mallards manager loves Northwoods gig," *Wisconsin State Journal*, July 22, 2004.

Chapter 8

Finkelmeyer, Todd, "Mallards' popularity downright shocking," *The Capital Times*, June 19, 2004.

Seligman, Noah, "Major makeover at Duck Pond," *The Capital Times*, June 8, 2004.

Thomas, Rob, "Bob, Willie concert set for August," *The Capital Times*, June 22, 2004.

"Changes on tap at Warner Park," *Wisconsin State Journal*, no byline, March 1, 2004.

"Bigger, better fits Mallards," *Wisconsin State Journal*, no byline, June 9, 2004.

"Duck Pond Upgrade: Mallards, city work together," *The Capital Times*, no byline, March 2, 2004.

Fishbach, Jeff, "Frk sets mark for longevity," *Wisconsin State Journal*, June 20, 2004.

"Board member: Chad Frk," *24Foundation.org* (Charlotte, N.C.), no byline, November 19, 2018.

"Madison Mallards offer another season of fun and games," *Wisconsin State Journal*, no byline, May 9, 2004.

Seligman, Noah, "Mallards fan wears his devotion with tattoo," *The Capital Times*, Aug. 11, 2004.

Masson, Jon, "Extra effort gives Mallards first title," *Wisconsin State Journal*, Aug. 15, 2004.

McMahon, Jason, "Champion Mallards aim to build," *The Capital Times*, Aug. 18, 2004.

"Handelsman steps down," *The Capital Times*, no byline, Sept. 11, 2004.

"Sports briefs: Handelsman to Fayetteville," *Wisconsin State Journal*, no byline, Oct. 8, 2004.

"Mallards hire new coach: C.J. Thieleke," *The Capital Times*, no byline, Oct. 12, 2004.

"NWL record 14 Current or Former Mallards selected in 2004 MLB draft," *Wisconsin State Journal*, no byline, June 24, 2004.

Davidoff, Judith, "Mallards eye spruce-up," *The Capital Times*, Dec. 11, 2004.

Anderson, Roger, "Even in the cold, Mallards heat up," *Wisconsin State Journal*, March 15, 2005.

Edes, Gordon, "Former Red Sox closer Radatz dies after fall," *Boston Globe*, March 17, 2005.

"Odds and Ends: Dick Allen at Duck Pond," *The Capital Times*, no byline, June 28, 2005.

"Ex-Mallard reaches majors," *The Capital Times*, no byline, July 14, 2005.

McMahon, Jason, "Love of the game drives GM," *The Capital Times*, Aug. 13, 2005.

"And the first shall be last, last shall be first," *Wisconsin State Journal*, Aug. 12, 2005.

"MVP Rogowski to ink pro deal," *The Capital Times*, no byline, Aug. 16, 2005.

McMahon, Jason, "No more room service, and no splits, either," *The Capital Times*, July 23, 2005.

"Fayetteville baseball coach recovering after grill explosion," WRAL-TV, June 11, 2012.

Pope, Thomas, "Fayetteville SwampDogs to remain in town at least through 2020 season," *Fayetteville (N.C.) Observer*, Jan. 29, 2013.

Chapter 9

Rathbun, Mary; McMahon, Jason; and Davidoff, Judith, "Mallards eye control of stadium," *The Capital Times*, Dec. 29, 2006.

Mosiman, Dean, "The Mallards talk of fancier digs," *Wisconsin State Journal*, April 28, 2006.

Winn, Luke and Hoyle, Dan, "Baseball Road Trip: The Blind Leading the Party," *SI.com*, June 25, 2006.

Baggot, Andy, "Mallards ask for input on new ballpark," *Wisconsin State Journal*, Dec. 29, 2006.

"2006: Record Fun at the Pond," *NorthwoodsLeague.com*, no byline, Aug. 17, 2006.

Eccher, Michael, "Former big leaguers, including Harmon Killebrew, give fans a thrill at Warner Park," *The Capital Times*, Aug. 5, 2006.

Kider, Teddy, "Still drawing huge flocks of fans," *The Capital Times*, Aug. 10, 2006.

Ziemer, Tom, "The Mallards look to rebound in the second half," *Wisconsin State Journal*, July 7, 2006.

Mertz, Adam, "Attracting a crowd," *The Capital Times*, Aug. 3, 2006.

Ziemer, Tom, "Mallards give fans lots to talk about," *Wisconsin State Journal*, April 27, 2006.

Mills, Adam, "Quote, Unquote," *Baseball America*, May 2007.

"Fifth lifts Mallards," *Wisconsin State Journal*, Aug. 7, 2006.

Joyce, Jason, "Mr. Mallard: General manager Vern Stenman's drive and vision are key to the team's success," *Isthmus*, June 8, 2007.

Bunke, Matt, "Marketing the Mallards," *Wisconsin State Journal*, May 13, 2007.

Gluskin, Michael, "Pride of the Mallards," *The Capital Times*, July 13, 2007.

Osborne, Jesse, "Duck Pond tops 1 million," *Wisconsin State Journal*, Aug. 10, 2007.

"First Hit: 5-4-49," *The Capital Times*, caption only for 2007 photo, March 11, 2015.

Oates, Tom, "Mallards' antics keep fans flocking," *Wisconsin State Journal*, May 31, 2007.

Conklin, Melanie, "'Webster' pitches in for Mallards promotion," *Wisconsin State Journal*, July 13, 2007.

Mulhern, Tom, "Major Mallard: Rockies' Ryan Spilborghs has a claim to fame," *Wisconsin State Journal*, July 15, 2007.

Hall, Sam-Omar, "North Side session tonight will focus on crime issues," *Wisconsin State Journal*, Aug. 20, 2007.

Yeater Rathbun, Mary, "Mallards' stadium project hits snag," *The Capital Times*, June 28, 2007.

DeFour, Matthew, "Planned reconstruction of the Warner Park stadium could cost $1.6 million more than expected," *Wisconsin State Journal*, Jan. 7, 2008.

Mertz, Adam, "Mallards stadium deal said to be close," *The Capital Times*, April 23, 2008.

Ziemer, Tom, "Mallards amping up all-star game display," *Wisconsin State Journal*, April 23, 2008.

Ziemer, Tom, "A life cut short," *Wisconsin State Journal*, May 18, 2008.

"Report Shows Heroin Caused Death of Player," *Washington Post*, compiled from news services, May 30, 2008.

Brown, Chandler, "Pitcher died of heroin overdose," *Atlanta Journal-Constitution*, May 31, 2008.

Zizzo, Nick, "Electric vibes at a damp opening win," *Wisconsin State Journal*, May 30, 2008.

"Food at the pond," *Wisconsin State Journal*, no byline, Aug. 6, 2008.

"Gary Coleman's first at bat as a Madison Mallard in the summer league Northwoods League," *YouTube.com*, 2008.

Simms, Patricia, "Duck Pond will get less of an overhaul," *Wisconsin State Journal*, Sept. 20, 2008.

"Mallards, city reach deal," *Wisconsin State Journal*, no byline, Oct. 29, 2008.

Chapter 10

Punzel, Dennis, "A 'circus' that pleases the purists," *The Capital Times*, May 22, 2008.

Mulhern, Tom, "Mallards have made some improvements, including a giant sandbox and a Bike Blind," *Wisconsin State Journal*, June 19, 2009.

"Nick Alsteen vs. Paul Molitor @ Duck Pond 2009," *YouTube.com*, 2009.

Mertz, Adam, "Ignitor still fires up fans," *The Capital Times*, Aug. 22, 2009.

"Around the Horn," *Wisconsin State Journal*, no byline, Oct. 1, 2009.

Cooney, Bill, "Stenman, Schmitt take on another project," *Wisconsin State Journal*, Dec. 17, 2009.

Shuda, Nathaniel, "Council Oks Northwoods team: Unnamed franchise will begin play in 2010," *Wisconsin Rapids Daily Tribune*, Dec. 16, 2009.

Polzin, Jim, "Madison Mallards timeline: 2000-2010," *Madison.com*, May 26, 2010.

Lucas, Mike, "Caloia invigorates Mallards," *The Capital Times*, July 14, 2010.

Polzin, Jim, "The Mallards always want to improve their fans' experience and this year is no different," *The Capital Times*, May 30, 2010.

Shafer, Scott, "Madison Mallards engineer the Duck Pond to meet the varied needs of their fans," *Wisconsin State Journal*, June 20, 2010.

"Negro Leagues celebration on deck," *Wisconsin State Journal*, no byline, June 22, 2010.

"Nathan 'Sonny' Weston—TheYNLBPTTravelingExhibit," *YesterdaysNegro-League.com* (click on "Gallery" then "A Negro League Experience" for video interview), 2010. youtube.com

Punzel, Dennis, "Overhaul set for Mallards' Duck Pond," *Wisconsin State Journal*, Nov. 7, 2010.

Goldstein, Richard, "Ryne Duren, Yankees Reliever Who Made Batters Nervous, Dies at 81," *The New York Times*, Jan. 7, 2011.

Polzin, Jim, "Now batting: The new Mallards," *Wisconsin State Journal*, Feb. 27, 2011.

Polzin, Jim, "From Pond to Palace," *Wisconsin State Journal*, May 15, 2011.

Punzel, Dennis, "New manager Greg Labbe has lots of enthusiasm and a winning background," *Wisconsin State Journal*, June 1, 2011.

Polzin, Jim, "Foul ball—The idyllic setting at Warner Park lacks one aspect so far this season: A first-place team," *Wisconsin State Journal*, July 23, 2011.

Moe, Doug, "Duck Pond might feel like Havana," *Wisconsin State Journal*, April 9, 2012.

Polzin, Jim, "Ducks not quite on the Pond," *Wisconsin State Journal*, May 27, 2012.

Polzin, Jim, "Playoffs are the genuine payoff," *Wisconsin State Journal*, May 30, 2012.

"Madison Mallards fan in green morph suit streaks," *YouTube.com*, 2012.

Punzel, Dennis, "Manager out after two seasons," *Wisconsin State Journal*, Aug. 23, 2012.

"Unique prizes planned for Mallards' 2 millionth fan Saturday night," *Madison.com*, no byline, July 14, 2012.

Obituary, Ronald E. "Ronnie" Reine, *Wisconsin State Journal*, June 7, 2012.

Ivey, Mike, "Madison Mallards serve up the winning pitch," *The Capital Times*, May 22, 2013.

Chapter 11

Ellison, Jack, "Ranger pick Scott a self-made slugger," *Tampa Times*, June 6, 1979.

Punzel, Dennis, "Familiar foe named manager," *Wisconsin State Journal*, Aug. 26, 2012.

Thomas, Katie, "Pitcher Who Injured Fan Is Given 30 Days in Jail," *The New York Times*, Aug. 6, 2009.

Polzin, Jim, "Change easy to see at always-changing Warner Park," *Wisconsin State Journal*, April 7, 2013.

Ivey, Mike, "The winning pitch," *The Capital Times*, May 22, 2013.

Polzin, Jim, "Environmentally friendly habits," *Wisconsin State Journal*, May 29, 2013.

Joyce, Jason, "Meet new Madison Mallards manager Donnie Scott," *Isthmus*, July 11, 2013.

Polzin, Jim, "Taylore Cherry is just beginning to scratch the surface of his talents during a summer in Madison," *Wisconsin State Journal*, July 18, 2013.

Moe, Doug, "Big leaguer's son finds own niche in game," *Wisconsin State Journal*, July 21, 2013.

Polzin, Jim, "Another feather in the cap: Joe McCarthy powers an offensive outburst as Madison wins its first title since 2004," *Wisconsin State Journal*, Aug. 17, 2013.

Reichard, Kevin, "Green Bay Bullfrogs bought by Mallards owners," *Ballpark Digest*, Nov. 19, 2013.

"Whiplash the Dog Riding Cowboy Monkey," *MallardsBaseball.com*, no byline, June 16, 2014.

"Whiplash the Cowboy Monkey," *YouTube.com*, 2009.

Glauber, Bill, "Kingfish step up to the plate," *Milwaukee Journal Sentinel*, May 24, 2014.

Temple, Jesse, "Madison Mallards don't duck away from zany promotions," *FoxSports.com*, April 24, 2014.

Kocorowski, Jake, "Madison Mallards a summertime hit for baseball-hungry fans," *SB Nation*, Bucky's 5th Quarter, June 15, 2014.

"Office Space Night with the Madison Mallards," *YouTube.com*, 2014.

Reichard, Kevin, "Big day for Big Top Baseball," *Ballpark Digest*, July 1, 2014.

Britton, Tim, "Mets prospect Peter Alonso is tearing through Double A while drawing some startling comparisons," *The Athletic*, May 30, 2018.

"Baseball Executive Vern Stenman Redefining Success Through Renovation," *Athletic Business*, AB staff, March 17, 2015.

Milewski, Todd, "Mallards management group negotiating to operate Breese Stevens Field," *The Capital Times*, Aug. 5, 2015.

Dopp, Alec, "Anthony Gonsolin: For the Love of the Game," *Northwoods-League.com*, July 9, 2015.

Uhlman, Harold, "Tony Gonsolin is Purring Along," L.A. Dodgers Chronicles, *LAdodgerschronicles.com*, May 18, 2022.

Uhlman, Harold, "Loons' Tony Gonsolin—'I just want to play baseball,'" *ThinkBlueLA.com*, Aug. 9, 2016.

Vanden Plas, Joe, "Talkin' baseball and more with Madison Mallards owner Steve Schmitt," *InBusiness* magazine, July 26, 2016.

Milewski, Todd, "Mallards' executives near deal to manage Breese Stevens Field," *The Capital Times*, Nov. 25, 2015.

Chapter 12

Popke, Michael, "Duck Blind, 2.0: A signature of summertime gets a green upgrade," *Isthmus*, March 30, 2017

Speckhard, Lisa, "New Mallards Duck Blind to cash in on latest architectural trend," *The Capital Times*, Jan. 8, 2017.

Mesch, Shelley K., "Team pitches renovation," *Wisconsin State Journal*, Jan. 8, 2017.

Mosiman, Dean, "2 new positions focus on violence," *Wisconsin State Journal*, Aug. 10, 2018.

Spedden, Zach, "Best Ballpark Improvement (Over $1M): Great Dane Duck Blind," *Ballpark Digest*, Oct. 6, 2017.

Milewski, Todd, "Duck Blind gets makeover," *Wisconsin State Journal*, May 28, 2017.

Milewski, Todd, "Donnie Scott is excited to coach a team that includes 17 freshmen," *Wisconsin State Journal*, May 30, 2017.

"Mallards in majors," *Wisconsin State Journal*, no byline, Aug. 20, 2017.

Becker, Abigail, "Breese Stevens operators look to draw soccer team," *The Capital Times*, Jan. 24, 2018.

Milewski, Todd, "Team takes cut at new approach to roster," *Wisconsin State Journal*, May 29, 2018.

Milewski, Todd, "Plantier a hit right from the start," *Wisconsin State Journal*, July 27, 2018.

Meyerhofer, Kelly, "Deluge shuts Shoe Box store down for a week," *Wisconsin State Journal*, Aug. 31, 2018.

"Mallards end relationship with Chick-fil-A, cite restaurant's support for anti-LGBTQ organizations," WKOW-TV, no byline, May 21, 2019.

"Mallards pro shop fire," *Wisconsin State Journal*, caption only, Oct. 19, 2019.

Milewski, Todd, "Breese Stevens set for spotlight," *Wisconsin State Journal*, April 26, 2019.

"Mets promote Alonso," *Wisconsin State Journal*, no byline, March 28, 2019.

"Scouts view 11 Mallards," *Wisconsin State Journal*, no byline, Aug. 7, 2019.

Stavenhagen, Cody, "Tigers prospect Justice Bigbie's sudden rise inspired by his mother, a 3-time cancer survivor," *The New York Times*, Feb. 19, 2024.

Petzoid, Evan, "How Detroit Tigers' Justice Bigbie went from 19th-round pick to doorstep of MLB debut," *Detroit Free Press*, Feb. 18, 2024.

"2019 Year in Review: Thank you fans!", *MallardsBaseball.com*, no byline, Aug. 16, 2019.

Jenkins, Wes, "Ducks on the Pond, Fans in the Stands," The Hardball Times, *tht.fangraphs.com*, Oct. 2, 2019.

Rovito, Rick, "Mills posts no-hitter in 15th big league start," Associated Press, Sept. 14, 2020.

Milewski, Todd, "Mallards, city will start look at future of Warner Park after finalizing extension to use agreement," *Wisconsin State Journal*, Dec. 15, 2020.

Milewski, Todd, "Boys of Summer won't play in Madison," *Wisconsin State Journal*, June 25, 2020.

Treleven, Ed, "Going ... going ... gone to the movies," *Wisconsin State Journal*, May 15, 2020.

Becker, Abigail, "City considering adjustment for Mallards," *The Capital Times*, Oct. 28, 2020.

Rogers, Jesse, "Chicago Cubs' Alec Mills tosses no-hitter," *ESPN.com*, Sept. 13, 2020.

Chapter 13

Schafer, Josh, "Vintage look for rebrand," *Wisconsin State Journal*, May 4, 2021.

Schoepp, Molly and Wondrash, Kevin, "Enjoying a 'Day at the Duck Pond,'" *Madison Catholic Herald*, Aug. 10, 2022.

Huynh, Kayla, "Samantha Rubin—Meet the Madison Mallards' first female general manager," *The Capital Times*, Sept. 14, 2022.

Kalk Derby, Samara, "Final buzzer for Rookies: June 30," *Wisconsin State Journal*, May 28, 2023.

Lucas, Mike, "As he did for Pete Alonso, Madison Mallards manager gets results," *The Capital Times*, July 11, 2023.

"Madison Sets Franchise Record, Beats Wisconsin Rapids," *Northwoods-League.com*, no byline, July 19, 2023.

Romano, Will, "325-gallon cocktail was a record-setting effort," *Wisconsin State Journal*, July 2, 2023.

"Best Ballparks Madison Mallards Review," *YouTube.com*, Aug. 14, 2023.

Rovegno, Susan, "Katy's First Baptist Church reaches 125th anniversary," *Katy Times*, Nov. 13, 2023.

Spreiter, Josh, "In the 608: What's new in 2024 at Warner Park," *Channel3000.com*/WISC-TV, May 28, 2024.

Crouse, Jake, "From carpenter to MLB hurler: Booser's wild journey to debut," *MLB.com*, April 19, 2024.

Lucas, Mike, "Madison Mallards coach is 'pumped' to play ball as season starts," *The Capital Times*, May 27, 2024.

Chapter 14

Liberman, Matt, "Madison Mallards to play as Motivational Speakers for Saturday night game," *Cllct.com*, July 1, 2024.

Arnold, Rory, "The Story Of Chris Farley's 'Matt Foley' Character, The 'Greatest Sketch In SNL History,'" *Ranker.com*, Sept. 23, 2021.

Chapter 15

Hirschberg, Dan, "Pinellas Park native reflects on MLB years; now manages in Wisconsin," *tbnweekly.com*, April 11, 2024.

ALSO FROM AUGUST PUBLICATIONS

Jim Gilliam: The Forgotten Dodger

The Baseball Thesaurus

The Football Thesaurus

The Complete Guide to Big League Ballparks

The Complete Guide to Spring Training

My 1961

The Right Thing to Do: The True Pioneers of College Football Integration

Raye of Light: Jimmy Raye, Duffy Daugherty, The Integration of College Football, and the 1965-66 Michigan State Spartans